THE NEGLECTED AUDIENCE

THE BROADCASTING DEBATE   5

THE NEGLECTED AUDIENCE

Edited by Janet Willis and Tana Wollen

BFI Publishing

First published in 1990 by the
British Film Institute
21 Stephen Street
London W1P 1PL

British Library Cataloguing in Publication Data
The neglected audience. – (The Broadcasting debate; 5)
  1. Great Britain. Broadcasting services. Audiences.
  Effects of policies of government. Great Britain.
  Government. Effects of policies on broadcasting. Services
  audiences
  I. Willis, Janet, *1948–*   II. Wollen, Tana, *1957–*
  III. Series
  384.540941

ISBN 0–85170–255–4

Cover design: Julia King

Typeset in 10 on 11pt Sabon by
Fakenham Photosetting Limited, Fakenham, Norfolk
Printed by
St Edmundsbury Press, Bury St Edmunds, Suffolk

Contents

Introduction

Janet Willis and Tana Wollen

At the heart of the current proposals to deregulate broadcasting in Britain lies a rhetoric about the individual's freedom to choose. 'The Government's aim is to open the door so that individuals can choose for themselves from a much wider range of programmes and types of broadcasting.'[1] Since the availability of television programmes will depend, to an increasing extent, on people's ability to pay for them, the airwaves, like gas, water and electricity, can no longer be considered as shared and regulated public resources.

These are not free choices. The range of services now available may be so destabilised as to make audiences bound to buy in to new systems. New aerials, dishes, decoders and subscriptions will make the present licence fee seem cheap at double the price. The increasing costs of advertising goods and services must also, in the end, be met by their consumers. Broadcasting will cost audiences more. The disappearance of a single, standardised fee means that information, education and entertainment will pass into more privatised realms of ownership and consumption. Television's contributions to a public culture will be divided between the information-rich and the information-poor. The wider choices are only available to those who can afford them.

As Eastern Europe opens its doors and considers the attractions of Western democracies, British television talks breathlessly of choice, the freedom to speak, the right to know. We would do well to examine the mechanisms of our own democratic processes, for the deregulation of broadcasting means that some of these are at stake. Democracy depends on information and debate being made widely available. The present duopoly is by no means perfect in this respect, but to differentiate access to public information according to the

1

capacity of citizens to pay for it will mean their correspondingly differentiated capacity to participate within a social democracy.

If the proposed legislation was intended simply to enable transnational television and channel multiplication, and to prepare and consolidate the domestic production base in order to facilitate indigenous production across the whole range of programmes, then it would not have aroused such concern. However, nearly 3,000 responses to the White Paper were submitted to the Home Office, most of them critical. The ITV network is already making adjustments to the diversity of its schedule. The ideals of public service managers and editors may seem so marginal to the business of television by the late 1990s, that the needs of audiences such as those considered in this volume, may have to be abandoned in favour of maximising ratings.

From some perspectives the viewer and the listener, as consumers of a wider range of channels, are indeed central to this government's broadcasting policy. Whatever their technological potential, the new delivery systems will be redundant unless viewers are prepared to pay for them. No wonder that the freedom to choose not to become a consumer is not being made to appear attractive. Unless television companies can deliver viewers to the advertisers who are to sustain their broadcasting, then they will not survive the rigours of an extremely competitive climate. Customising their channels to more particular tastes and interests, television companies will have to attend to ever more fragmented clusters of viewers. It is a more particularised notion of viewers, as a collection of individuals, which is emphasised in the proposals for change. It is the notion of an audience, as people holding something in common for the length of a programme or an evening's schedule, which is being neglected.

A deregulated market for broadcasting implies the end of the notion of a vulnerable audience, requiring patrician protection from the 'great and the good'. The market will be sustained by audiences 'robust' (in Peacock's view) in their purchasing activity. Nevertheless, it is hard to see how the market will be able to deliver its promises, and how the new structures will be able to please more people for more of the time. It is most likely that television's responsiveness to viewers will be framed solely in marketing terms. To an increasing extent, it will be the interests of advertisers, not viewers, that television will have to serve.

From this perspective, the central place of viewers and listeners in the government's policy is usurped, as the Consumer Association pointed out in its response to the White Paper: 'Here there is no contract at all between the viewer and the provider of programmes: the contract is between the company and the advertisers. The

2

amount advertisers are willing to pay reflects what they estimate to be the likely popularity of the programmes.... The advertiser has absolutely no direct interest in the maintenance of a diverse and varied programme schedule of high quality – which we have defined as crucial to the maintenance and promotion of real consumer choice....'[2]

Paradoxically, the 'wider range' promised threatens the loss of a variety, which, again paradoxically, enables a degree of cultural and social cohesion. How often will television surprise, provoke, or enlighten audiences when they are so able to tailor their choices, if the box in the corner delivers only what has been ordered, what is expected? How often will viewers be able to 'catch' something quite by chance, if more channels simply support fewer kinds of programmes? 'Suppose pay-as-you-go TV comes in?' asks one viewer. 'I'll only ever pay for the things I know I like, and I'll never learn anything new!' (quoted by Samantha Cook on p. 53 of this volume).

At the moment, this variety in programming is charged to audiences at a uniform rate, costing each household no more each day than the price of a tabloid newspaper. Viewers of all kinds constitute audiences for the diversity of programmes currently available. 'There is a difference of at most one percentage point as between ABC 1s and C 2 D Es across the whole range of programming types. Given the way all other forms of cultural participation are heavily canted in socio-economic class terms, this is a major achievement and a major contribution to the creation of a common culture and a common citizenship.'[3]

In this volume our aim has been to provide an insight into how people have considered themselves as members of particular audiences, and how those audiences have been considered by others. The opening section deals with questions about a generalised television audience: how it is researched; how it has gained access; how, in the light of Channel Four's provision for 'minorities', television has had to come to terms with different views of the audiences it serves. In the following sections the particular audiences considered constitute the majority of those who watch television most and who will be least able to pay for the new 'choices': children, the elderly, black people, the disabled and the poor.

The writing here has various sources. The perspectives and tones of these pieces speak as powerfully as the arguments they put forward. They are based on academic research, on personal experience, on marketing campaigns. They reveal some of the varied requirements people make of television. Some make cautionary, if not gloomy forecasts; others are confident in the 'robust' critical faculties which television audiences exercise. The only consistent view of television here, across the many expressed, is of its vital, cohesive role in the social fabric. How broadcasting legislation will affect the textures and patterns of that fabric remains to be seen. What this volume makes clear, however, is that politicians and broadcasters are not the only people qualified to judge.

Notes

1. *Broadcasting in the 90s: Competition, Choice and Quality* (HMSO, 1988), para. 1.2.
2. Quoted in *Responses to the White Paper*, edited by Wilf Stevenson and Nick Smedley (London: British Film Institute, 1989), p. 28.
3. Nicholas Garnham in *Life After the Broadcasting Bill* (Manchester Monographs, 1989), p. 22.

Behind the Ratings: The Politics of Audience Research

David Morley

More channels, video recorders, remote controls, and programmes around the clock have prepared British audiences for a wider selection from television, even before the airwaves are deregulated. Yet, while broadcasters may be hesitant to admit it, the means of measuring audience choices are woefully inadequate. BARB (The Broadcasters' Audience Research Board) has recently been described by one commentator as a 'slow moving Leviathan', its meter panel producing 'data bearing little resemblance to viewing'. As cheaper technology, multiple sets and extended programming are seen to make viewing increasingly a matter of individual choice, the industry is 'stuck with a system measuring the views of the household'.[1]

So far, the main response to these criticisms has been to engage in an increasingly frantic search for a 'technical fix'; for 'better' technologies of audience measurement. Since it began measuring TV audiences in the USA in the 1950s, Nielsen has been able to tell when sets in a sample household are on and to what channels they are tuned. The problem has been to determine who in the family is watching at a given time. A few years ago, Nielsen introduced the 'people meter' to provide that information by requiring viewers to push a particular button whenever they are watching television. The meter was also devised partly as a response to AGB's (Audits of Great Britain) attempt to break into the American audience research business. Now dissatisfaction with that technology has led to the development of the 'passive people meter' – a computerised, cameralike device attached to each set in the household, which uses an 'image recognition' system to identify who is actually present in front of which sets, and when.[2] What we have here is the attempt to provide a technical 'solution' to the problems of TV audience research. Is the problem amenable to this kind of solution? Developing 'better' techniques for data gathering can only solve certain types of problems.

The kind of clinical empiricism which has dominated audience research for years substantially involves processes of methodological isolation and abstraction and has led media research up too many blind alleys.[3] In pursuing a dynamic which is basically overdetermined by the discourse of 'ratings', this kind of research has consistently mistaken rigour for understanding. Ratings discourse describes viewers and the differences between them, exclusively in terms of a few generalised and standardised viewing behaviour variables. All other bases of identity and difference are ignored. Thus the subjective element is minimised and 'watching TV' is reduced to the observable behaviour of having the set on. This is further assumed to be a simple act, having, in principle, the same meaning and salience for everybody.

This is simply a misleading picture of the activities involved. Improved techniques of audience measurement are certainly needed, but so are improved methods of audience research. We need to measure not only what different types of audience do, but also to discover how and why they view as they do. Such an approach would involve an understanding of television viewing as a complex activity within a domestic context. However, it would be fruitless to pretend that this debate is simply an academic one, concerned only with questions of epistemology and methodology: to attack the ratings is to attack the economic and political heart of the television industry.

Television institutions need to 'know' their audience if they are to survive. The diverse forms of 'knowledge' that are generated by techniques of audience research are then circulated within the business through a range of reports, presentations, etc. From this perspective then, a television audience is not so much a real group of people as a discursive term which lumps people together only in so far as they have an observable activity, 'watching television', in common.[4] The real complexities of audiences' tastes and choices are simplified in the coherent vision which ratings give the industry. Ratings solve a fundamental problem: the need to measure and 'know' a dispersed and varied audience. Ratings thus convert an elusive occurrence (people watching television) into calculable units on which economic transactions can be based, for audience measurement provides the economic foundations of the broadcasting industry.[5]

6

'People-watching-television' are taken to be the basic units of audience measurement. These people are, of course, singular and subjective and all located in particular circumstances, but inclusion of the details of their singularity would of course make the production of ratings impossible. Their individual and subjective differences have to be suppressed in order to create calculable categories of ratings, emphasising averages, regularities and generalisable patterns rather than idiosyncratic differences.

Predominant modes of television audience research do not, in fact, usually measure television viewing as such: they measure some other factor (the set being on, presence in the room) which is then assumed to be a reliable indicator of viewing. They also assume that switching the television on is an index of wanting to view the specific programme turned to (rather than, for instance, a reflex action signifying 'getting home'). There are a number of the problems hidden behind this assumption, not least the common use of television as an excuse to escape the demands of domestic interaction, regardless of whether attention is actually being paid to the screen. Viewing is often presumed to be the result of an individual's decisions, whereas we know that it often takes place in groups, where power is unequally distributed, and choices must be negotiated. For many viewing is quite often 'enforced': they put up with what someone else in the group wants to watch, rather than leave the room (even in multi-set households, there is usually a 'main set', which is the focus of competing demands). The predominant modes of audience research often take decisions to view out of context, and make the import of each decision the equivalent of any other. This means that the significance of other factors such as the unequal access which different viewers have to televisual technology, to the knowledge often required to get the most out of programmes, or simply to domestic space, is ignored. These gaps in audience research persist, even though we know, at the simplest level, that watching television is not a singularly-focused activity and that not everyone engages with television in exactly the same way.

Gunter and Svennevig quote surveys showing variously 50 per cent and 64 per cent of viewers claiming to watch television while usually doing something else at the same time.[6] Having the set on, or the presence of people in front of the set can mean, 'a hundred different things'.[7] Taylor and Mullan quote a number of their respondents reporting that they put the set on when they come into the house as automatically as they might switch on the lights.[8] Having the set on is, for many people, simply an index of 'being at home': they don't necessarily have any intention of watching it.[9] Similarly, Collet and Lamb's research shows that the people in their sample were only in the room for about 80 per cent of the time the television was switched on and only spent around 65 per cent of that time looking at the screen at all. They note baldly that 'informal interviews with the subjects failed to reveal any consistent meaning for the term "watching television"', and go on to conclude that 'watching cannot be quantified' since 'there is no way of knowing whether someone who has his eyes glued to the screen is "viewing" any more intently than a man who is ostensibly conversing with his wife. Although the first person's eyes are on the screen, his thoughts may be far away, and while the second person's eyes are oriented to his wife, he may actually be listening to what is happening on television'.[10] Viewing figures can neither indicate the different levels of attention people in front of a TV set pay to it nor assess the attention that people within its earshot might be paying to the soundtrack.

The head-counting which is fundamental to the whole ratings enterprise is based on the simple binary opposition of watching/non-watching TV. However, in the face of all the research evidence quoted above, it can no longer be assumed that having the TV set on equals watching, nor that watching equals paying attention, nor that watching a programme implies watching the 'commercials' in it. Television watching is increasingly recognised as a complex and variable mode of behaviour, characteristically interwoven with other, simultaneous activities. The simple binary 'watching/non-watching' opposition which is the epistemological basis of all the ratings statistics begins to break down under the weight of all the variables which need due consideration. With some justification, Ien Ang argues that 'the project of audience measurement may have reached a point of no return: it may have definitively lost its hold on its basic assumption: namely, that watching TV is a simple type of behaviour that can be objectively measured'.[11]

If we take this argument seriously, then the kind of research that needs doing would involve identifying and investigating all the differences hidden behind the catch-all category of 'watching television'. We all watch television at different times, but with how much attention and with what degree of commitment, in relation to which types of programmes and occasions? If these kinds of qualitative distinctions could be established then the aggregated statistical results of large-scale survey work could be broken down into meaningful components. Research needs to investigate the complex ways in which television viewing is embedded in a whole range of everyday practices, and how it partly constitutes those practices itself.[12] How particular communications technologies come to acquire particular meanings and how they come to be used in different ways, for different purposes, by people in different types of household also needs to be researched. We need to investigate television viewing and the rules of its 'accomplishment') in its 'natural' setting: as Silverstone and I have argued elsewhere, the household or family, as the basic unit of domestic consumption, offers the most appropriate context for the naturalistic investigation of the consumption and production of televisual (and other) meanings.[13]

Images of the Audience

British broadcasting has always imagined its audience predominantly as a 'family audience'. The audience addressed is presumed to be composed of nuclear family households, and this image remains absolutely pivotal to programming, scheduling and public policy for the regulation of television, even though the nuclear family accounts for a shrinking minority of households in the UK.[14] In our current research at Brunel University,[15] we are attempting to explore how television (among other communications technologies) is actually used in a sample of nuclear families from different economic and cultural backgrounds. However, research also needs to be done on the place and use of these media within single-parent families and single-person households since these are increasingly common. We also need to research the non-domestic use of television and video technologies as they percolate the public spaces of bars, clubs and shopping precincts. Only then can we begin to form a clearer picture of what television really signifies in its everyday context.[16]

A key issue is how broadcasting links public and private domains. In so far as it cuts through the boundaries of the family or household and its private universe, it is a potentially disruptive and 'dangerous' force. From this point of view, the basis of the state's role in regulating broadcasting's potential disruption of the family was most clearly defined in the deliberations of the Annan Committee, 'People watch and listen in the family circle ... so that violations of the taboos of language and behaviour ... which exist in every society, are witnessed by the whole family ... in each other's presence ... These violations are more deeply embarrassing and upsetting than if they had occurred in the privacy of a book, or in a club, cinema or theatre.'[17]

In the terms of this argument, the family (and specifically, children within the family) needs protecting. Indeed it is the figure of the child (and specifically, the 'unsupervised' child of the working-class family) which is ideologically central.[18] Television generates such a paedocratic image of its adult audience as ('child-like') that concern with the upbringing and moral welfare of future citizens ultimately legitimates a whole range of state interventions into broadcasting

9

policy, the debates around 'video nasties' and 'broadcasting standards' providing cogent examples. I want to suggest that it is within this ideological framework that contemporary debates about the television audience need to be placed.

Demographic, Cultural and Technological Change

We now face the simultaneous (and interactive) effects of two sets of changes – changes in family structure (and culture) and changes in communications technologies. Only 13.8 per cent of households in the UK conform to the classic stereotype of the nuclear family of the *Janet and John* literature. Furthermore, there is an overall increase in the number of single person households (now 23 per cent overall and particularly high among the elderly), and a decline in the average number of children in the family (down from 3.09 in 1961 to 2.63 in 1983). Overall there is a growing fragmentation of family and household types, a much higher percentage of married women going out to work (34 per cent of all households; around 60 per cent of households containing married women), and a much higher rate of divorce (up from 40,000 per annum in 1960 to 160,000 per annum in 1984) and of remarriage (by 1982, 34 per cent of all marriages involved at least one partner who had been previously married). The number of single-parent families is also growing (up to 5 per cent of all households, by 1984), a significant proportion of them in difficult economic circumstances.

At the same time many commentators have noted a strong tendency in the UK towards the development of a more thoroughly 'privatised' or 'home-centred' culture,[19] with a major shift of expenditure towards the home and a shift in leisure patterns towards home-based activities. The difficulties of public cinemas over the last few years, in contrast to the growth of the home-based video market bear witness to these shifts.[20] The overall decline in 'out-of-home' leisure activities (with only the more affluent and highly educated minority of the population showing any tendency to move against this trend) means that the study of television use, along with other forms of domestic leisure, becomes all the more critical if we are to understand the patterns of life and leisure adopted now by the majority of Britain's population.

If we turn to the second set of changes referred to above, we see a fundamental transformation in the nature of broadcasting. Writing just over ten years ago one commentator noticed: 'In its [fifty] year history, the role of the TV receiver has not changed at all. Its sole function is to show programmes distributed from a central point for mass consumption ... essentially TV is as it was when the BBC first started broadcasting from Alexandra Palace.'[21] While the TV set often remains the 'family hearth', it is now the potential pivot of a video/entertainment/computer facility and the significance of the 'box in the corner' has utterly changed.

Technological changes have social effects. The trends towards both multi-set (and multi-VCR) households raise important questions about their implications for patterns of domestic life, 'Will families, through increased reliance on TV for different kinds of entertainment, be drawn closer together by this common source of amusement ...? Or will there be a trend towards the increased acquisition of TV sets and accessory equipment (e.g. video recorders, home computers, etc.) with each family member having access to a "personal home entertainment" system which they can use privately, resulting in increased isolation of family members from each other?'[22] There are certainly those in the industry who support the implicit hypothesis: 'Whereas in 1980 TV was a family mechanism, it now provides a more personal service for each of the various members of the household. Consequently, specific segments and programmes are now being identified as the sole domain for various discrete audiences.'[23]

It may well be that this particular analysis overstates the extent of change; none the less, in the context of so many associated and concurrent changes, in demographic patterns, cultural trends and in the communications technologies themselves, a number of our working assumptions about television and its audience(s) need to be considered afresh.

If television is a domestic medium, then the full implications of its complex domestic context have only just begun to be researched. The insistent focus of this research has, in the first instance, been descriptive and (principally) ethnographic. It has moved away from the emphasis on the 'causes and consequences' of television viewing, posing instead detailed questions about what that viewing involves and how it gets done in different contexts. Given that television is a domestic medium, it follows that the appropriate mode of analysis must take the unit of consumption of television as the family or household, rather than the individual viewer. This means considering individual viewing patterns within household relations and to insist that individual viewing activity only makes sense within these relations. Here we begin to open up a whole set of questions and differences hidden behind the indiscriminate label of 'watching television'; differential modes of viewing engaged in by different types of viewers, in relation to different types of programmes shown in different slots in the overall schedule, in relation to different spaces within the organisation of domestic life.

11

Redefining Television Audience Research

Thus far, I have argued for the importance of recognising (and researching) television as a medium operating in a domestic context. However, that recognition alone is not sufficient. Television should now be seen as one of a number of information and communication technologies; as part of a domestic media 'ensemble' alongside the video, the computer, the telephone and the answering machine, as well as the walkman, the stereo and the radio. This is to recontextualise the study of television in a broader framework, in order to understand its domestic uses and significance in the contexts of contemporary technological and consumer culture. It is to understand how particular technologies are domesticated, how they are taken up and used (both materially and symbolically) in different ways in families and households of various types. This in turn means considering how the physical structure of the home has determining effects. In crowded households for instance, watching TV may be a strategy adopted to defuse tension, as individual members use the set to create their own private 'space', substituting aural for physical walls.[24]

Communications technologies are not to be understood as having a fixed set of 'properties' which somehow then have 'effects' on their users. Some lead 'double lives', as they come to be used for entirely different purposes from those for which they were originally designed. This is not to romanticise the 'freedom' of the consumer: the user's choices are of course influenced by how these technologies are advertised and marketed. The point is to understand how constraint and creativity are played out in different circumstances. The telephone answering machine may be used in one family to make the household's external boundary more permeable, while in another it may be used (perhaps at key moments, such as mealtimes) to protect the household's privacy. Similarly, in a multiple-set household everyone may gather together around the 'main set' for certain types of 'ritual' viewing (the News in one household, *Neighbours* in another), while in another everyone may watch the same episode of *Neighbours* but on separate sets, in separate rooms. We don't yet understand how or why television, along with the other communications technologies has come to mean such different things to different people. In my view, it is only by means of detailed, empirical and largely ethnographic work, which is sensitive to the various dimensions of television's domestic context, that we shall better understand these processes. This is not simply some matter of micro-sociology or anthropology. When television and other media enable us to become increasingly international in our outlook, we need to pay close attention to the domestic communication practices

12

through which people come to understand their positions as members of households, interest groups, regions and nations.[25]

Notes

1. John Billett, quoted in *Broadcast*, 15 June 1989.
2. For recent trade commentaries on these issues see W. Freeman, 'Watching the Watchers', *Broadcast*, 14 July 1989 and P. Kleinman, 'The Electronic Countdown', *The Times*, 19 July 1989.
3. See M. Wober, 'Psychology in the Future of Broadcasting Research', *Bulletin of the British Psychological Society* 34, 1981; see also R. Silverstone, D. Morley et al., 'Families, Technologies and Consumption', Discussion Paper, Centre for Research in Innovation, Culture and Technology, Brunel University, 1989, for a further discussion of the methodological issues at stake.
4. I am grateful to Ien Ang for allowing me to draw extensively here (and also below) on material from her new book *Stalking the Viewer in the Wild* (London: Routledge, forthcoming).
5. See Ang, *Stalking the Viewer*, for a fuller development of these arguments; see also John Harley, 'Invisible Fictions', in *Textual Practice* vol. 1, no. 1, 1987 for another perspective on the TV audience as a discursive construct; see also Dallas Smythe on 'the audience commodity', in his *Dependency Road* (Norwood, N.J.: Ablex, 1981).
6. B. Gunter and M. Svennevig, *Behind and in Front of the Screen* (London: John Libbey, 1987).
7. B. Towler, then Head of the IBA's Research Dept, made these points in his presentation to the Royal Television Society, Cambridge, 1985.
8. L. Taylor and B. Mullan, *Uninvited Guests* (London: Chatto and Windus, 1986).
9. See R. Kubey, 'TV Use in Everyday Life', *Journal of Communications* vol. 26, no. 3, 1979.
10. P. Collet and R. Lamb, *Watching Families Watching Television*, report to the IBA, 1986.
11. Ang, *Stalking the Viewer*.
12. See P. Scannell, 'Radio Times: Temporal Arrangements of Broadcasting in the Modern World', in P. Drummond and R. Paterson (eds.), *Television and its Audience* (London: BFI, 1988); see also J. Lull (ed.) *World Families Watch Television* (Beverly Hills and London: Sage, 1988).
13. See D. Morley and R. Silverstone, 'Domestic Communications: Technologies and Meanings', to appear in *Media, Culture and Society* vol. 12, no. 1, 1990; R. Silverstone 'Television and Everyday Life', in M. Ferguson (ed.) *Public Communication: The New Imperatives* (Beverly Hills and London: Sage, forthcoming).
14. R. Paterson, 'Planning the Family – the Art of the Schedule', *Screen Education* no. 35, 1980; D. Cardiff and P. Scannell, 'Broadcasting and National Unity', in J. Curran (ed.) *Impacts and Influences: Essays on*

Media Power in the Twentieth Century (London: Methuen, 1987); C. Brunsdon and D. Morley, *Everyday Television: Nationwide* (London: BFI, 1978).

15. 'The Household Uses of Information and Communication Technology', a project under the direction of R. Silverstone, Centre for Research in Innovation, Culture and Technology, Brunel University. The project is funded by the ESRC (Economic and Social Research Council) as part of its research programme in Information and Communication Technology.
16. See R. Kubey, 'TV use'; see also E. Medrich, 'Constant TV: a Background to Daily Life', *Journal of Communication* vol. 26, no. 3, 1979; D. Leamish, 'The Rules of Television Viewing in Public Places', *Journal of Broadcasting* vol. 26, no. 4, 1982.
17. Proceedings of the Annan Committee, 1977.
18. R. Paterson, 'Family Perspectives in Broadcasting Policy', paper to BFI Summer School, 1987.
19. See A. Tomlinson (ed.), *Consumption, Identity and Style* (London: Routledge, forthcoming); see also the various reports of the Henley Centre for Social Forecasting for further interesting data in this field.
20. D. Docherty et al., *The Last Picture Show?* (London: BFI, 1987).
21. A. Burkitt, quoted in F. Webster and K. Robins, 'Mass Communication and Information Technology', in *Socialist Register* (London: Merlin Books, 1979).
22. See B. Gunter and M. Svennevig, *Behind and in Front of the Screen*.
23. *Marketing Review*, June 1987, p. 15; quoted in Paterson, 'Family Perspectives'.
24. T. Lindlof and P. Traudt, 'Mediated Communication in Families', in M. Mander (ed.), *Communications in Transition* (New York: Praeger, 1983).
25. C. D. Rath, 'The Invisible Network: TV as an Institution in Everyday Life', in P. Drummond and R. Paterson (eds.), *Television and Its Audience* (London: BFI, 1988).

Opening Up the Box

Giles Oakley

Much has been made of the idea of 'consumer choice' in relation to television, of broadcasting as akin to a marketplace with an ever-growing range of 'products' on offer. What is striking is how seldom those discussions have considered the value of Access TV, which might be seen as the ultimate in consumer choice, giving viewers themselves power to determine the specific, detailed content of a programme. Access TV has existed for well over a decade and a half, but somehow only at the margins: it is probably seen as peripheral even among its own supporters and admirers. While it is not one of those make-or-break issues that fuel the controversies about broadcasting in the 90s, as the epitome of a certain kind of public service broadcasting, its future should not be allowed to pass into history without some scrutiny.

'Access' involves some notion of the public, the non-professional broadcaster getting on to the airwaves. To some, it can mean phone-in programmes, like the BBC's current *Open Air* audience-reaction programme, or the video-box element in Channel Four's *Right to Reply*.

To purists, however, the term 'access' always meant programme-making in which real power, including editorial control, is handed over to a group or to an individual outside the broadcasting institutions. The philosophy behind access in this sense seems to have been developed first in North America in the 1960s and early 70s in projects like New York's *Open Channel*, WGBH in Boston's *Catch 44* and Canada's *Challenge for Change*. At the heart of these programmes was a critique of mainstream broadcasting, which influenced Access TV in Britain because it struck a chord here. It was summed up in these surprisingly mild terms by one of those involved

15

in WGBH's *Catch 44*: 'If the professionals alone continue to determine how society will be reported and reflected, they may go on excluding, quite unconsciously, many of the views, life-styles and community backgrounds different from their own.'[1]

As the post-war consensus weakened in Britain in the early 1970s, there was a growing sense that the traditional terms of 'balance' in broadcasting too easily excluded many views and experiences. The American experiments provided an impetus to programme-makers in Britain, at a time when debates about whose voices should be heard on television were hotting up, inside the BBC and in the political parties. One of those who was most responsive inside the BBC was Rowan Ayres, Editor of the long-running 60s series, *Late Night Line Up* (later simply *Line Up*). This was a late-evening live chat and discussion show on BBC 2, which was usually studio based, allowing responses to the night's output or other topical issues. The *Line Up* team was much impressed by *Catch 44*, which since 1970 had been operating a first-come, first-served studio open to the public in Boston. They were also influenced by Professor George Stoney of the New York Alternative Media Centre, who was invited to discuss his work on *Line Up*. Stoney used a mobile video van, with a single reporter/camera-operator who would hand a microphone to people in the street. These American developments inspired the tentative experiments taking place in Britain. On one unplanned occasion in 1971, *Line Up* took a film camera to a Guinness factory canteen to get the views of the workers there on various TV programmes. The presenter, Tony Bilbow, found himself repeatedly challenged by the workers' views that the BBC weren't *really* interested in the views of ordinary viewers, that the film would be edited to make it say what the BBC wanted it to say. The result was that *all* the film was shown on *Line Up*, unedited, clapper-boards and all.

That incident eventually led to the establishment of *Open Door* in 1973, the first major access series in Britain, under Ayres' editorship. As described by *Radio Times*, *Open Door* was a slot where 'people and groups are given a chance to have their own say in their own way'. The programme's internal guidelines decreed that air-time should be given to 'views or activities which are not presented on the air in the course of other programming'. There had been other British experiments including local cable TV like Swindon Viewpoint in the early 1970s, and on network television there was *Open Night*, a studio discussion hosted by Granada's Mike Scott. In 1972, Tyne Tees TV in Newcastle presented a 10-minute film from SOCEM (Save our City from Environmental Mess) followed by a balancing studio discussion. But *Open Door* swiftly became the flagship for access, leading to the creation of the BBC's Community Programme Unit

16

which in turn produced numerous other access or neo-access series, such as *Write On*, *Grapevine*, and the teenagers' series *Something Else*.

The format for *Open Door* was film and/or studio and people were allowed to take over complete editorial control, enabling them to say whatever they wanted, within the limits of the law. That very freedom was a source of anxiety both inside the B B C and elsewhere, Rex Winsbury reported in *Campaign* in April 1973:

> When the idea of the *Open Door* programme was first announced, there were some prominent Tories, some in office, who were saying (in private) that they were not as worried about sexual licence on the programme ... as they were about political licence. It might become, they said, an open door for every extremist, revolutionary and subversive clique to propagate its views – a golden opportunity to get access to the mass media and to preach their dangerous gospels – an opportunity that they would never otherwise get.

Open Door lasted for a decade, its resources and budgets gradually increasing and earning respect inside and outside the industry. There were a number of programmes which created controversy, including, in the 1970s, ones by the Campaign to Stop Immigration, the Campaign for Nuclear Disarmament and Palestine Action. All the big rows were political, and most involved the institutional role of the B B C itself, because every time a politically sensitive programme was chosen for *Open Door* it raised questions about who did the choosing and why. The most troubling questions, however, were those raised in programmes made by groups questioning the broadcasters themselves, such as the Campaign Against Racism in the Media's *It Ain't 'Alf Racist Mum* in 1979. Any assessment of how free access broadcasting can be compared with mainstream has to take account of those institutional pressures on the commissioning department not to rock the boat.

In 1983 *Open Door* was replaced by *Open Space*, which has continued at intervals ever since and is still the flagship of access on the B B C. The budgets have been increased and the surface qualities of professional programme-making skills have improved, even though they are still comparatively low-budget productions. Some regret the passing of the rough-edged, raw quality of the early, unpredictable programmes, many of which were 'live' studio presentations. *Open Space* operates in a similar way to *Open Door*. A production team, budget, the necessary resources and equipment are provided to the 'accessee' who can exercise full editorial control if desired. Some programmes are made in partnership with the CPU (Community Programme Unit), or 'on behalf' of the accessee, if they don't have the time or inclination to get deeply involved on a day-to-day basis. Editorial control can be exercised by the accessee through *every* stage of production from planning, scripting, filming and editing.

By the time *Open Door* had become *Open Space* the access philosophy had spread far beyond the BBC, contributing to the creation of Channel Four in 1982 in a very direct way. Several individuals who were prominent in the new Channel or who made programmes for it had worked in the CPU, including Paul Bonner and Mike Bolland. Early series like *Whatever You Want* (RPM for Channel Four) were spawned by the CPU notions of access.

In Channel Four's remit was the duty to cater to hitherto neglected audiences. Here was official recognition that whole sections of public opinion had been excluded from access to the screen. Channel Four responded by widening the range of voices to be heard on television with *Opinions*, *Right to Reply*, *Comment* and *Diverse Reports*, each in its own way allowing access of a kind. *The Eleventh Hour*, which started in November 1982, drew on the best of independent film and video-making, giving some challenging and experimental work wider exposure. In September 1983, *People to People* was launched. 'Whatever the method used,' wrote Caroline Spry in 1986, 'the crucial idea at the heart of *People to People* is that of collaborative production: the making of television programmes with and by members of a community which truly reflect their ideas and experiences and not that of the professional programme-makers.'[2]

Back in the BBC by the late 1980s, the staple fare of *Open Space* had been augmented by the occasional series *Split Screen* on BBC 2 which brought together two authored films from opposing viewpoints. On BBC 1, the series *Network* gave a platform to viewers to criticise TV programming or broadcasting policies. Both signalled an expansion of the ways in which access could happen.

Alongside these developments in the 80s, the phrase 'Independent Access' acquired a new meaning when independent production companies fronted by IPPA (Independent Programme Producers' Association) lobbied for access for themselves. Not, it has to be noted, for sections of opinion or for points of view from the audience or from society at large. Their campaign had unprecedented success, culminating in both the BBC and ITV being obliged by the Government to take at least 25 per cent of their production from independent companies.

The Independent Access campaign merits attention. One of its claims held that Independent companies, some of which inherited or appropriated the cultural cachet associated with the old-style 70s 'independent' film companies, would bring a rich diversity of new production techniques, new programme ideas, new faces, new voices. This was, of course, demonstrably true: Channel Four did, indeed, achieve many of those things (often, it has to be said, with ex-BBC and ITV staff). Another side of the Independent Access argument however can mean the privatisation of *Kilroy* on BBC1 in 1989: what had been an entirely in-house production was put out to tender, with no diversification of production or of voices heard. However, the independent claim was a powerful one, compared with the comparatively marginal impact of access, because it had Government support behind it.

The pressure of the campaign was not premissed on intentions of opening up the airwaves to more points of view, but on opening up markets, and breaking the power of the old duopoly. It was an economic case, clothed not by the Government, but by the growing numbers of freelance programme-makers and independent producers, in the rhetoric of cultural enrichment, freedom and diversity.

In retrospect, the campaign had an astonishing triumph, both for the speed of its success and the unchallenged nature of its ideological pitch. The old duopoly gave in with hardly a whimper. What was left out of the independent companies' arguments for their own access were the older ideas about access for audiences.

Those original ideas were based on a notion of empowerment: *Open Space*, for example, aims to give airtime to the 'un-represented, the under-represented, or the mis-represented'. While Access TV in a looser sense has proliferated, and minorities in society are better catered for than they were, media power still remains in comparatively few hands. The underlying power relations are largely unchanged, and political agendas are still set by those who never dream of resorting to an access programme to get their message heard. If the impact of access has been limited however, and the commanding heights of broadcasting largely unchanged, we now face the prospect of even greater concentrations of power shifting away from publicly accountable bodies to purely commercial operations. In the existing broadcasting institutions, access has made most headway in the BBC and Channel Four, both bodies where the public service ethic has been strongest. How well access survives in the bracingly competitive 90s may depend not on any public service obligation, but on the fact that for much of its history Access TV has been cheap TV. One of its weaknesses hitherto may give it an unsuspected strength. Connoisseurs of clumsy, live studio presentations in the style of *Open Door* circa 1973 may be on the threshold of a Golden Age.

Notes

1. Chris Dunkley, 'Open Door', *Financial Times*, 5 April 1973.
2. *The Work of Channel Four's Independent Film and Video Department* (Channel Four, 1986).

Making a Difference: The Impact of Channel Four

Alkarim Jivani

'Broadcasting is not for programme-makers but for audiences. What is perhaps most important about Channel Four is that we try to think of our viewers as individuals with individual tastes and judgements, viewers who make individual choices. Viewers today do not want a centralised conformity; they want choice. They want difficult issues debated, want to hear the other side of the argument; expect programmes presented from different points of the political spectrum, understand that an opinion is not necessarily the opinion of the programme, not of the channel, but only of the individual expressing it, understands his or her right to express that opinion even if not everyone agrees with it, understands that we are all different with different tastes and are each entitled, on various channels, to find our own different satisfactions in the democracy of broadcasting.'

Jeremy Isaacs[1]

When Isaacs uttered those words in his valedictory speech in the 1987 Edinburgh Television Festival, his message was received with approbation not only by the broadcasters he was addressing but also by politicians and the press who only five years earlier had attacked Isaacs for putting exactly those principles into practice. In the intervening time the notion that television need not address itself to everybody all the time had become not only acceptable but positively desirable – an indication of how the Channel has challenged and changed the way broadcasting is thought about and practised.

21

It has been part of Channel Four's *raison d'être* that it should be different from the other channels in four specific ways. Firstly, it should be different in its structure and the way it sources its programmes. Secondly, that experimental formats and new modes of televisual expression should be encouraged. Thirdly, that the programmes it produces should address those issues which fall between the cracks on the other channels. Finally, and most important of all, Channel Four should address special interest groups with programmes targeted specifically at them.

The blueprint for the nascent channel appeared in an article by Anthony Smith in the *Guardian* in April 1972. Smith argued that the new channel 'would supplement existing broadcasting by broadening input, by allowing anyone to bring a project to it, whether an independent programme-maker with a finely worked out plan, neatly costed, or a firm, organisation or individual with merely a well-argued complaint that some issue was failing to get across to the public'.

The idea was picked up by the Annan Committee in its 1977 report which recommended that the new channel should 'say something new in new ways' and that it should be run by something called the Open Broadcasting Authority which would not produce any programmes itself but act as a publisher commissioning others to deal with programme-making. The Labour government of the time viewed this favourably but the Conservative government which took power in 1979 felt rather differently. William Whitelaw, the minister in charge, liked the idea of programmes for and by minority interest groups, but he also wanted strict safeguards. The result was that the channel emerged as a curious amalgam of liberal ideology and the new ideas of a market-led environment which established themselves in the late 70s. This paradox was reflected in the channel's mode of production which turned left-leaning programme-makers into small businessmen who had to live by their entrepreneurial skills.

With these laudable intents Channel Four came on air in the Autumn of 1982 to almost universal opprobrium. Many of its brave new programmes received audiences which were so low that they could not be measured and so received a zero rating. Headlines like 'Channel Snore' and 'Channel Bore' began appearing in the press. Within the Channel Four offices the phrase 'Storm over Four' was used as a catch-all term to describe the torrent of articles in the tabloids. Isaacs also used the phrase for the title of his book about the first five years of Channel Four as a private joke.

It seemed in 1982 that the four principles described above on which the Channel had been built would not provide a secure foundation. Its method of sourcing was leading to complaints from programme-makers who argued that commissions from Channel Four weren't steady enough to maintain a healthy and vibrant independent sector. The experimentation in terms of content and format was leading to criticisms about boring and badly produced programmes, and the lack of measurable viewers led to accusations that Channel Four was targeting itself at minority groups which either didn't exist or didn't want to watch what Channel Four had to offer.

Even the Channel's best friends were forced to admit that some of the programmes which were put out in the opening days and weeks were amateurish and gauche. 'I wanted to ensure that somehow new ideas, wonky ideas maybe even, by conventional wisdom, bad ideas ... would be put forward as to how we should operate and what we should put on air. I was after a combination of professional experience, or relevant but disparate disciplines and of innocent experience if there was invention to go with it.'[2] Unfortunately not many politicians and opinion formers saw it that way.

Seven years later those early doubts about whether the four principles on which Channel Four was built have been largely dispelled. Not only is the Channel seen as an unmitigated success but its innovations have also been emulated by the more established broadcasters. Furthermore the Channel Four mode of operation is being seen as a possible blueprint on which to base new channels which might appear in a deregulated future.

Let us begin with programme production. One of the most innovative aspects of Channel Four when it began was its structure – there were no large studios, no central facilities, no edit suites and no cutting rooms. In short, no programme-makers. Instead the channel acted as a publisher, commissioning various 'authors' to produce work which could then be presented to the consumer under one unifying imprint.

Up until then broadcasters had produced everything in-house with the exception of films and foreign programming. Before the advent of Channel Four there were next to no independent programme-makers, now there are at least 700 who, between them, are producing 2,500 hours of broadcast television a year, a figure which is expected to rise by 60 per cent to reach a minimum of 4,000 hours by 1991.[3] This rise in the number of independent programme-producers and their access to the airwaves is largely attributed to the government's decision to use the Channel Four model to introduce an element of the free market to the BBC and the ITV companies with the decree that both organisations should source 25 per cent of their original output from outside by 1992. The government is also considering the idea that the proposed fifth channel should be set up

along the same lines as Channel Four, without any in-house programme production and thus drastically reducing the costs of
launching the channel.

Channel Four's unique structure for sourcing programmes has
been matched by the structures and formats of the programmes
themselves starting with the station logo. Although it may look
unremarkable now, the station logo set a new standard when it was
made. So much so that Martin Lambie-Nairn, the designer, had to go
to America for the computer graphics since nothing of the sort was
available in Britain. Since then the Channel Four logo has had a far
reaching influence spawning many rip-offs and even a parody in the
form of a television commercial for Hamlet cigars. There have been a
myriad of other technical advances not only in specially created slots
where experimental work which tinkered with the grammar of video
and television was given an airing but also in the mainstream of
programming.

These include single camera Beta-cam shoots, almost unheard of
ten years ago; the robotic image of the actor who played Max
Headroom with graphics swooping all around his head and a myriad
of other examples. Quite often programmes combined innovative
content with format in a way which made the two inseparable. Sylvia
Harvey cites the example of *They Haven't Done Nothing Yet* in
which a dub poet declaims directly to the camera.

> The combination of boldly opinionated comment, poetic language
> and direct address shifts the boundaries of that mode of expression
> which is the documentary genre, as well as adding to the repertoire
> of forms available for expression. At the level of content because
> this is the speech of a black person ... something is added to the list
> of contents.[4]

This is true of many Channel Four programmes which were innovative both in style and in content, making it difficult to delineate the
two strands. *Brookside*, for instance, had no parallel when it first
started in that instead of using studios it was filmed entirely on a real
housing estate bought for the purpose, with camera-work which
seemed more like *vérité* cinema than soap. In terms of content, it
tackled contemporary subjects in a gritty manner which questioned
the parameters of soap opera. Until then issues such as abortion and
homosexuality were taboo in twice-weekly serials but after *Brookside* these could not be ignored. The look, style and storylines of *East
Enders*, for instance, owes much to its Channel Four predecessor
which had set a precedent in going for gritty, urban storylines and
shooting them on a set made up of real buildings rather than flats.

Perhaps Channel Four's most daring act was to make a virtue out of a format which the rest of the broadcasting establishment regarded as anathema: the talking head. *Opinions* and *Comment* both allowed individuals to have their say on a nationally networked channel by speaking directly to the audience. Far from being dull, as had been predicted, both have produced some memorable contributions. Individuals burning to say something were not confined to these two slots. Even though one of the philosophical corner-stones of British broadcasting has always been the notion of public service television, until the advent of Channel Four, the industry was loath to face its public and give serious consideration to how it might make itself accountable to viewers.

A number of Channel Four's founding team felt that television was grossly and pitifully[5] defensive over its mistakes and were determined to involve viewers to a greater degree than had hitherto been possible. So the Video Box, a booth with a camera which allowed viewers with a gripe to have their say, were installed in several cities and the results were shown on *Right to Reply*, the televisual equivalent of a newspaper letters page.

Since this was the only conduit for public discussion of broadcasting, Channel Four decided to extend its remit to cover programmes broadcast by all channels. The BBC took the message and launched the monthly *Network* and the daytime programme *Open Air*, both of which provide a forum for programme discussion by viewers.

In terms of addressing special interest groups, Channel Four's remit was to fulfil the needs which could not be met anywhere else. Instead of addressing itself to a broad family audience as all the other channels tried to do, Channel Four was charged with appealing to minorities. In this context the word 'minority' is used loosely to include all sorts of special interest groups. There were programmes for gardeners, anglers, wine-lovers and other groups who had never been targeted before. Most notable of all there is S4C, the Welsh Fourth Channel, which is a separate entity, partly funded by Channel Four, set up to provide programming for Welsh speakers, speaking to them in Welsh.

Young people who had been all but ignored on the other channels have been given a succession of programmes aimed primarily, but not exclusively, at youth audiences. Pop music programming, which, before Channel Four, was confined to *Top of the Pops* and *The Old Grey Whistle Test*, and next to nothing on the ITV network, was given a shot in the arm with *The Tube*. Comedy programming like the hour-long pieces by the *Comic Strip* in Channel Four's opening season, gave the alternative comedians of the early 80s pride of place.

Interestingly the BBC now has a department for youth programmes, which had never been considered necessary in the past, and a specialist youth slot in *DEF II*. Similarly *Channel Four News* has provided an hour-long, mid-evening analytical news programme aimed at those who find the half-hour bulletins on the other channels too shallow. People with a special interest in the media were given *Open the Box* and subsequently *The Media Show*. Foodies have been served up with programmes which do more than merely deliver a succession of recipes, which had been the pattern of cookery programmes in the past. Strands like *Take Six Cooks*, *Cooking with Mosimann* and *Mushroom Magic* have opened up the genre in a way which would have been difficult to imagine before the advent of Channel Four, but which seems commonplace now.

In addition to minority interest groups, Channel Four has been in the forefront in serving groups bound together by race, gender or sexuality. Up until 1982, the needs of Asian and Afro-Caribbean viewers were entirely marginalised by broadcasters. Only the BBC made any sustained effort to reach these communities and then the programmes were produced with a sense of duty rather than enthusiasm and pushed to the edge of the schedules.

Until the arrival of the *Bandung File*, even Channel Four was not brave enough to put programmes aimed at ethnic goups into primetime but it did pour more resources into making programmes for these communities than ever before. There were magazine programmes for Asian and Afro-Caribbean communities which have since been joined by *Orientations*, a programme for Britain's Chinese community. In addition there were programmes on popular Indian cinema and special video projects like the Black Audio Film Collective's *Handsworth Songs*. There have also been fictional strands like *Tandoori Nights* and *Desmond's* which use black actors and are set within the black community.

This in turn has had a knock-on effect on other broadcasters and the BBC in particular, which also launched new magazine programmes aimed at Asians and Afro-Caribbeans, and what's more transmitted them near peak viewing times.

Programmes and films of special interest to gay men and lesbians have been a regular feature of Channel Four schedules even though in some cases, notably Derek Jarman's *Sebastiane*, this led to opprobrium being heaped on the channel. In 1989, *Out on Tuesday*, the first networked series aimed at this group, was successfully launched. In the past, despite the fact that there are more gay men and lesbians than dog-owners in this pet-loving nation, no broadcaster had been convinced of the need for a regular programme for this section of the population.

Admittedly Channel Four's approach to some minority groups has not always been well-received by viewers in general or even the groups at whom that programming is aimed. There is research which demonstrates that viewers are critical of the Channel's approach. A recent study by the Broadcasting Research Unit showed that 61 per cent of adults didn't believe that there should be any programmes aimed at homosexuals.[6] The report also discovered that, unless closely questioned, some Afro-Caribbean viewers did not see Channel Four as substantially different from ITV which, given the channel's aim of serving ethnic minorities, is disastrous. The report also discovered that having a lot of regular access to television is not particularly important to Asians and Afro-Caribbeans – less than half wanted programmes aimed at their ethnic group. Although respondents were not questioned about this specifically, the implication is that black people would prefer to see more black faces on *Brookside* and other mainstream programmes rather than have them boxed off into a ghetto slot. Interestingly, the authors of the study argue that although viewers may not themselves want to watch programmes aimed at a variety of special groups, they approve of the idea.

In a fascinating and curious way the public appears to believe in Channel Four the way that it believes in some abstract concept like 'truth'. People continue to tell lies despite holding 'truth' to be an ultimate value and they want Channel Four to be committed to the culturally and politically disenfranchised even though the majority will never watch such programmes.... In a very profound way, the public believes in the channel as an expression of the need for television to challenge, renovate and, occasionally, disturb.[7]

The question is: how will the impending changes in the British broadcasting industry impact on Channel Four and what ramifications will they have on the Channel's ability to challenge, renovate and disturb viewers? The main motivation behind the proposed change is the perceived need to liberalise the broadcasting industry and to remove what are regarded as monopolies and entrenched interests. In these terms, Channel Four's current position is seen as monopolistic. The Channel has a guaranteed income from the ITV companies which pay 17 per cent of advertising revenue to Channel Four and S4C. In return the ITV companies are allowed to sell Channel Four's airtime to advertisers. While this gives ITV monopoly rights to the sales of television advertising, it has its advantages too – the chief one being that Channel Four is freed from direct commercial pressure, so rather than worrying about ratings it can

27

concentrate on programming and more specifically meeting its programme remit.

This situation is seen as anti-competitive by the government which has come under pressure from free market lobbyists and advertisers to sever the connection between ITV and Channel Four. Should ITV and Channel Four have to compete with each other, the minority channel would be forced to go into a ratings war with its rival pitting drama against drama and quiz show against quiz show. Alternatively the strategy would have to be for Channel Four to compete with ITV not by matching it but by providing programmes which would deliver the audiences ITV fails to reach.

However, if Channel Four did that, it would only be able to survive in its present form so long as advertisers were prepared to pay as much, or more, for specific sub-groups on Channel Four than they pay for the mass market audiences delivered by ITV.

There is, therefore, a tension between the commitment to a free market in broadcasting and Channel Four continuing to produce innovative programming which may, in some cases, be unprofitable to make. The Government has rejected calls to privatise the channel and announced its intention to set up a public trust. Channel Four will, however, sell its own advertising time in competition with ITV (Channel 3). Although Channel 3 will be obliged to make 'cross announcements', the wording falls short of the 'cross promotion' currently enjoyed and suggests that the relationship between the channels will be more competitive than complementary. In addition, the Government has indicated that there should be a minimum income set for Channel Four (equivalent to 14 per cent of the net advertising revenue) and if revenue falls below this target by up to 2 per cent Channel 3 will pay the difference. Equally, if advertising revenue rises above the 14 per cent level then half that revenue will go to Channel 3 and the other half will be retained by Channel Four. By this slender thread the commercial channels are tied together in the hope that Channel 3 will have enough of a stake in Channel Four not to indulge in a ratings war.

The Government seems to accept that Channel Four is a valuable and distinctive element in British television culture which we would lose at our peril. But when the channel assumes responsibility for its own advertising, will some of the minority audiences it currently serves be threatened as they prove to be unattractive target groups for advertisers? Finally, will these elaborate financial mechanisms be enough to guarantee Channel Four's distinction, if its independence is jeopardised by government approval of corporation members?

Notes

1. 'Cheerio Chaps, I'm Off...', a speech to the Edinburgh Television Festival given by Jeremy Isaacs, 30 August 1987.
2. J. Isaacs, *Storm Over Four. A Personal Account* (London: Weidenfeld and Nicolson, 1989).
3. IPPA (Independent Programme Producers Association), *Members Directory 1990.*
4. S. Harvey, 'Deregulation, Innovation and Channel Four', *Screen* vol. 30, nos. 1/2, Winter/Spring 1989.
5. Liz Forgan in an interview with *The Times*, 16 September 1982.
6. David Docherty, David E. Morrison, Michael Tracey, *Keeping Faith? Channel Four and Its Audience* (London: Broadcasting Research Unit/ John Libbey, 1988).
7. Ibid., p. 75.

THE LOW PAID

Our Necessary Luxury

Barbara Vickers

I have been a lone parent for nearly seven years. When I was first on my own I had two toddlers and one on the way. We lived in an isolated spot where the highlight of the week was talking about the weather to the milkman. In those days I had a very old black-and-white set. It was a real companion. The first year of my single parenthood coincided with the birth of breakfast television, and the set would go on first thing in the morning so that Frank Bough and Selina Scott would seem as though they were really there talking to me and I could enjoy some adult company. With breakfast TV I found I could do without my habitual daily paper, and anyway I knew deep down I was never going to win the Bingo.

The old set kept breaking down and I decided to put some of the money saved on newspapers towards a colour TV. Everyone I knew had a colour set and I decided that watching *Rainbow* in black and white wasn't really educational for my young family.

As people change, so do their needs. We moved house and as my children got older I had the chance to think about more than household chores. Having rested the grey matter for several years I discovered a new use for my companion in the corner – the Open University. My dependence on the daily quota of soaps diminished as I discovered all kinds of interesting programmes.

The children's needs have also changed. They all now love the wildlife documentaries and take in all sorts of wonders. Of course, they take the little box in the corner for granted and laugh at me when I tell them we would have to get a black-and-white set if anything happened to the one we've got. They also think I'm joking when I wonder how we will pay the TV licence which gets harder every year, not because it goes up all the time but because we are caught in a poverty trap which is hard to escape with three children.

30

Since a close friend won a satellite TV the children keep asking me to try and win one too, since they know I'll never buy one. They seem to like the idea of getting up at 5 a.m. to watch cartoons. Well, I've never been lucky in competitions and fortunately we don't know many people with one of those plastic triffids on the side of their house. We occasionally have a clash of wills when there is a programme on that I think is unsuitable for them to see. The protesting will often go on for days as the children list all their friends who were allowed to watch the programme in question. It's tough when I always seem to be saying 'No' to them. 'No, you can't buy this or that,' and 'No, you can't watch that,' but at the end of the day it's not the TV that rules.

What has become a real strain on us are the cult programmes for children which have very expensive spin-off toys. It is difficult for young children to understand that there simply isn't enough money in the piggy bank to buy today's cult hero, complete with vehicle, and that even Santa has limits. I must admit that I try to steer them away from all the advertising on TV mainly so that when I go shopping I can be the one to choose what goes into the basket, instead of having to veto all the junk food they have seen advertised and have been brainwashed into wanting. It is this kind of extra pressure which puts up the cost of viewing without our realising it.

I am aware that some households live quite happily without a TV, presumably because they don't have any of the pressures that are created by having one. Remarks occasionally bring to light the fact that our ancestors lived contentedly enough without television, but is it fair to make such a comparison? Surely today's standards should be set by those who have at least a reasonable standard of living. After all, the Victorians may well have made their own entertainment but they generally had large families and lived in large houses. Nowadays, we lead more isolated family lives, often in tiny houses with relatives spread across the country. While today's children have more leisure time than previous generations many parents are reluctant to let their children play outside since there are so many violent crimes being committed.

There can be no denying that my family gets its money's worth from television at the moment. Although we all know how to switch it off we nevertheless watch a fair amount between us. Where else could I take the children for entertainment, and how else could I give them education out of school that would cost so little for four people? Its advantages far outweigh the disadvantages. As a lone parent I simply couldn't manage without our set.

31

Screening Out the Poor

Peter Golding and Graham Murdock

Information and communication facilities are a central resource for the effective exercise of citizenship in liberal democratic societies. Accordingly, ensuring a reasonable degree of equity in public access to strategic information and communications resources has been a central policy goal. These resources include both facilities directly relevant to individuals, particular circumstances such as access to advice on welfare, consumer and legal rights, and to a telephone, as well as access to the more general flows of information and analysis which enable people to understand and evaluate the options for public policy and to make rational political choices. Consequently, the conditions of access have implications not only for the quality of life and political capacity of individuals but for the vitality of democracy as a whole.

The importance of television in most peoples' leisure time, and as a major source of the images and information with which they construct their understanding of the world around them, has never been greater. Terrestrial broadcasting continues to dominate domestic leisure time and new technologies both singly and in combination are moving the television screen to the hub of an increasing array of social, economic, and cultural activities.

This poses with renewed vigour questions of equity in the distribution and availability of communication resources. In this chapter we consider the implications of recent and impending shifts in the political and economic arrangements governing both broadcasting and other industries exploiting the domestic importance of the television screen.

Equity is generally seen as having an economic and geographical dimension. The working principle has been that nobody should be unreasonably excluded from basic information and communications resources on the grounds of either income or area of residence. Historically, this objective has been pursued through a variety of mechanisms. They include the provision of a substantial infrastructure of publicly funded information and communication services, most notably the public library and public broadcasting systems. There have also been public subsidies to voluntary sector initiatives in information provision: law centres, consumer advice centres, welfare rights centres, citizens advice bureaux, community information networks. Finally, regulations have governed the geographical reach and pricing of basic information facilities such as telephone services for which the customer pays directly.

Over the last decade, these mechanisms have been increasingly called into question. Public policy has moved towards a greater emphasis on the commercial or tradeable value of information and on the need for customers to pay for the resources they consume, with renewed encouragement for private sector initiatives in information provision and a corresponding reduction in the level of public subsidies.

By altering the established balance between public-sector, voluntary-sector and market provision, and by changing the terms on which these sectors operate, these initiatives raise important new issues of access and equity. They also raise central questions for the future quality and vitality of democracy, since the commercialisation of information and communications provision has coincided with welfare and fiscal policies that have significantly widened the income gap between the poorest sectors of the population and the rest, excluding large numbers of people from access to even the most basic communications facilities.

The Growing Divide: Income Differentials and Communications
Where communications facilities are obtainable only at a price, then the range of disposable incomes determines differential access to these facilities. The growing gulf between low and high income households over the past decade has created a consumer society in which patterns of consumption are massively unequal. Between 1979 and 1985 the poorest twenty per cent of households had to endure a drop in their living standards, after allowing for tax and cash benefits, of six per cent. In 1988, 5.73 million full-time and 4.18 million part-time workers were paid below the Council of Europe's 'decency threshold', a rise of over 2 million people since 1979. In the same period the average earnings of the highest paid tenth increased by 161 per cent in gross money terms.[1]

Tax and benefit changes between 1979 and 1989 delivered just four per cent of the net proceeds to the poorest 18 per cent. The numbers in receipt of social security have soared while many benefits have declined in real value. By 1987 8.35 million people in 5.01 million households were receiving Supplementary Benefit, an increase of over one-third since 1983. The 1986 Social Security Act, followed by the 1988 budget, and now the vastly regressive poll tax have all exacerbated these developments.[2]

The consequence of these movements in income distribution has widened the gap in the expenditure choices and patterns of different groups in the population. Low income groups have a lower consumption elasticity for service goods, including leisure and communications resources, than higher income groups: their income is more substantially committed to the necessities of food, fuel, clothing, and housing. As Table 1 shows, despite the relative evening of the gradient produced by the flat-rate television licence fee, on most communications goods expenditure is sharply differentiated by income.

TABLE 1

Weekly expenditure on communications goods and services among selected income groups

Weekly Income (£)	Expenditure on (£)		
	TV/video/audio equipment	*Books/newsp'rs magazines*	*TV/video rental/licence*
60–80	0.57	1.51	1.73
100–125	0.91	2.00	1.72
150–175	2.73	2.46	2.16
225–250	4.51	2.98	2.08
325–375	5.33	3.50	2.31
550+	10.19	5.54	2.50

Source: Family Expenditure Survey 1986 Department of Employment, 1988. Table 1

The outcome of this pattern is illustrated in Table 2 which clearly shows that, although virtually all households have a TV set of some kind, ownership of newer screen-based technologies is severely limited among low-income groups and that a third of those in the lowest income band do not even have a domestic telephone.

From Public to Private: The Citizen Turns Consumer
The emerging market-oriented communications system addresses people primarily in their role as consumers, firstly of the communications goods and services they buy directly, and secondly of the

34

TABLE 2
Ownership of communications and information facilities among households in selected income groups

Weekly Income (£)	Percentage owning:			
	TV	Telephone	Video Recorder	Home Computer
60–80	96.9	67.4	12.6	3.3
100–125	98.1	76.7	21.2	7.6
150–175	97.7	76.3	31.6	9.6
225–250	97.5	87.3	43.5	21.2
325–375	98.0	94.1	56.5	26.5
550+	98.4	98.2	64.8	28.8

Source: Family Expenditure Survey 1986 Department of Employment, 1988. Table 1

products promoted by the advertising which helps finance some of the new services they offer. In the process it marginalises or displaces a range of their identities, in particular the identity of citizen.

The starting point for most modern British discussions of citizenship is T. H. Marshall's essay, *Citizenship and Social Class*, written in 1949.[3] Marshall distinguishes three basic dimensions of citizenship – civil, political and social – and traces the development of the rights associated with them together with the institutions that promote and guarantee them. Civil rights are centrally concerned with an individual's freedom of action within the sphere of 'civil society'. They include: freedom of speech; freedom of thought and religion; freedom of movement and association; and centrally, the freedom to own and dispose of property. Property rights are assigned a pivotal role in classical liberal theory, as the major guarantor of individual choice. In this conception the market is ambiguously the sphere of liberty which the state threatens to erode whenever it goes beyond its assigned 'nightwatchman' role of regulating the use of force and overseeing the legal system that guarantees individual rights. As the then Home Secretary, Douglas Hurd, recently reiterated, for Conservatives 'private property is the natural bulwark of liberty'.[4]

Political rights are concerned with the conditions under which people participate in the exercise of political power, by holding public offices, by electing members of the national and local bodies which formulate policies and pass laws, and by involving themselves in the exercise of those laws through membership of a jury. The image of the citizen as a participant in the political process is of course central to classical conceptions dating back to Ancient Greece. It is what separates a citizen from a subject. The latter may have the right to protection under the law, but only citizens can take part in determining the nature of the laws by which they will consent to be governed.[5]

Marshall sees the social rights of citizens as the distinctive product of the twentieth century. His presentation of them centres on the struggle to secure a basic standard of life and wellbeing for all through the institutionalisation of the welfare state. For the purposes of the present argument we need to add the rights of universal access to communications and information facilities. These emerged at the same time and were underwritten by public provision funded out of local and national taxes and institutionalised through the organisations responsible for continuing education, public libraries and, later, public broadcasting. Although Marshall does not stress the importance of communication rights, they are presupposed by his general definition of the social rights of citizenship as covering 'the whole range from the right to a modicum of economic welfare and security to the right to share to the full in the social heritage and to live the life of a civilised being according to the standards prevailing in the society'.[6] This definition involves a substantial widening of the traditional conception of citizenship. It is no longer simply about participation in the political process, it is also about the conditions which allow people to become full members of the society at every level.[7]

Although Marshall does not prioritise these three dimensions of citizenship, it is clear from the overall thrust of his argument that he sees social rights as the essential precondition for political participation and for full social membership. To put it another way, poverty is a powerful mechanism for excluding people from these entitlements.[8] Marshall was writing in 1949, after the Labour Government elected in 1945 had pushed through the reforms that completed the creation of the modern British welfare state. He had good reason to think that this restructuring was an irreversible step towards securing the basic resources for citizenship. Forty years on, with the experience of a decade of radical conservative administrations headed by Mrs Thatcher to assimilate, it is clear that this optimism was premature, and that these resources have been progressively eroded.

In principle we can identify three main kinds of relations between communications and citizenship. First, people must have access to the information, advice and analysis that will enable them to know what their rights are in other spheres and allow them to pursue them effectively. Second, they must have access to the broadest possible range of information, interpretation and debate on areas that involve political choices, and they must be able to use communications facilities in order to register criticism, mobilise opposition, and propose alternative courses of action. And third, they must be able to recognise themselves and their aspirations in the range of representations on offer within the central communications sectors, and be able to contribute to developing these representations. These rights in turn imply that the communications and information system should have two essential features: at the level of production it should offer the maximum possible diversity of provision and provide mechanisms for user feedback and participation; at the level of consumption it should guarantee universal access to the services which can ensure the exercise of citizenship regardless of income or area of residence. Can these essential communicative resources for citizenship be guaranteed by a production and distribution system that is increasingly organised around market mechanisms? Our answer has to be 'no', at least not given the present organisation of the relevant markets and the distribution of income.

Whenever access to the communications and information resources required for full citizenship depends upon purchasing power (whether through customer payments or through the unequal distribution of advertising subsidies to production), substantial inequalities are generated which undermine the nominal universality of citizenship. As we noted earlier, income differentials have widened considerably under the three Thatcher governments. At the same time the communications and information system has been progressively 'privatised' and the public sector eroded and commercialised. As a result, the poor suffer from a double disadvantage. They are priced out of the markets for new services and left with an infrastructure of public provision which is either unable or unwilling to provide the full range of resources for citizenship.[9]

Towards the 'Pay-Per' Society
The present shift towards what Vincent Mosco has called the 'pay-per' society,[10] produced by a decade of privatisation policies, has very significant implications for peoples' access to strategic communications services. The effects can be clearly seen in the area of telecommunications, which has already travelled down the road on which television services are about to embark.

The telephone is the hub of most peoples' interpersonal information system. It connects them with the informal networks offered by friends, neighbours and relatives, and provides a major point of access to the professional information services of organisations like Citizens' Advice Bureaux, voluntary and community groups, and welfare rights agencies. However, some of the groups most in need of support and advice are among those least likely to have access to a domestic telephone. According to official figures, in 1986 some 36 per cent of lone senior citizens living on a state pension had no phone. Among households with a weekly income of under £45, the figure rises to 52 per cent.[11] Even those with a phone in the house may find their use of it inhibited by the relatively high cost of making local calls, produced by British Telecom's policy of rebalancing its charges to attract business users.

The difficulties facing the poor are further compounded in the case of value added services. As a result many of those most able to benefit from these facilities are least able to obtain them. Home shopping provides a case in point. The ability to order goods from home and to have them delivered to the door would be particularly valuable for pensioners and the disabled. Yet experience to date clearly shows that such schemes will only reach those in need if there is extensive public subsidy. Where they are run on a straightforward commercial basis they are geared to service the better-off, extending the advantages they already enjoy.

Screening Out the Poor

Television services are about to follow the same path. As advertising and viewer subscription become the major sources of finance so choices in this new multi-channel market-place will be relatively expensive. Historically, British broadcasting has been built around a notion of public service which sees television as a public resource that should speak for and to the full range of social experiences and interests. It should be available equally to everyone, regardless of their level of income or area of residence. This idea was financially underwritten by the BBC receiving the whole of the compulsory licence fee levied on the possession of a television set, and the Independent Television (ITV) companies have exclusive rights to sell advertising on ITV and Channel Four in their franchise areas. This historic commitment to universal service will be weakened when the new broadcasting legislation begins to take effect.

Taking into account the cost of the licence, the cost of the set and the indirect costs of advertising, the average household pays around £210 a year to watch BBC, ITV and Channel Four in colour.[12] Adding any one of the new clusters of services – VCR, cable or Direct Broadcasting by Satellite – involves doubling this figure, which puts these options well beyond the reach of most low-income households.

As Table 2 shows, contrary to popular stereotypes, video recorders are a relatively rare fixture in poorer households, with only 12.6 per cent of those in the lowest income band having one, compared to 64 per cent of those with a weekly income over £550 and 44 per cent of those with an income over £225. Moreover, even

38

if a machine is rented rather than purchased outright, running it in the normal way will cost about £230 a year.

Nor is subscribing to one of the new cable systems a much cheaper way of extending options for viewing. In mid 1988, it cost on average just over £214 a year to buy into cable services, which is still more than twice the price of basic broadcast services. The final costs of access to the satellite-delivered services offered by Sky and BSB via a domestic dish reception are not yet clear, but they are very unlikely to be less than the costs of a cable hook-up and may well be more.

Given these prices, television watching in poorer households will be restricted to basic broadcast services, though exactly which services will remain accessible to all is now open to question, as we move towards the 'pay-per' system sketched in the Government's 1988 White Paper on broadcasting.[13] Although for the moment the BBC will continue to be funded mainly out of the licence fee, the government looks forward to its eventual replacement by its intention to encourage the progressive introduction of subscription on the BBC's television services (White Paper, para. 3.10). To accelerate this process, increases in the licence fee after 1991 will be fixed below the general rate of inflation (rather than being indexed to it as at present), forcing the BBC to seek other sources of income to cover the shortfall.

Some of the services provided by the ITV companies and by the new Channel 5 will also be funded by direct customer payments, though it will be up to each individual operator to decide on the exact mix of subscription and advertising. They will also be free to decide what to show and when to show it, and although they will be required to offer 'a diverse programme service calculated to appeal to a variety of tastes and interests' (White Paper, para. 21), they will be under no obligation to offer the full range of present programming. As the Peacock Committee recognised very clearly, some of the programmes most at risk in this new environment are the programmes most central to sustaining communicative resources for citizenship in its broadest sense (para. 561–570).

Unlike the Independent Broadcasting Authority which supervises the ITV system, the new overseer body for commercial television services, the Independent Television Commission, will operate with a 'light touch', prioritising the growth of television services as a business, rather than defending or extending broadcasting as a public service in pursuit of diversity.

Conclusion
We have argued that a shift to a more market-orientated provision of information and communication goods is emerging at a time when

the ability of different groups in the population to dispose of their income on these goods is being markedly distinguished by widening gaps in income and wealth. This exacerbates tensions between the actual operations of markets and the promise of full and equal citizenship. Markets present the freedom to choose among competing products as the central and defining liberty of the modern age. But the right to purchase or not to purchase cannot be equated with the right to participate in determining the rules which regulate market transactions, nor with the right to organise in pursuit of changes in the distribution of strategic resources. In any case, as we have noted, for many people in contemporary Britain choices in the communications marketplace are purely nominal since they lack the economic means to translate their needs and desires into purchases. Where material inequality massively differentiates people's access to the goods and services necessary for citizenship, then political rights are the victims of the vicissitudes of the market place and its inegalitarian structure.

Notes

1. Low Pay Unit, *Ten Years On: The Poor Decade* (1989).
2. P. Esam and C. Oppenheim, *A Charge on the Community: The Poll Tax and the Poor* (Child Poverty Action Group, 1989).
3. T. H. Marshall, *Citizenship and Social Class* (Cambridge: Cambridge University Press, 1950).
4. Douglas Hurd, 'Citizenship in the Tory Democracy', *New Statesman*, 29 April 1988.
5. A. Vincent and R. Plant (eds.), *Philosophy, Politics and Citizenship: The Life and Thought of British Idealists* (Oxford: Basil Blackwell, 1984).
6. Marshall, *Citizenship*, p. 11.
7. D. S. King and J. Walron, 'Citizenship, Social Citizenship and the Defence of Welfare Provision', *British Journal of Political Science*, vol. 18, no. 4, pp. 415–443.
8. P. Golding (ed.), *Excluding the Poor* (Child Poverty Action Group, 1986).
9. G. Murdock, 'Poor Connections: Income, Inequality and the Information Society', in Golding, *Excluding the Poor*, pp. 70–83.
10. V. Mosco, 'Introduction: Information in the Pay-Per Society' in V. Mosco and J. Wasko (eds.), *The Political Economy of Information* (Madison: University of Wisconsin Press, 1988).
11. Office of Telecommunications, *Report of the Director General of Telecommunications* (London: HMSO, HC 432, 1988), Table 2.3, p. 71.
12. B. Ball, 'The Rising Cost of Small Screens', *Broadcast*, 28 April 1989, p. 23.

13. Home Office, *Broadcasting in the '90s: Competition, Choice and Quality* (md 517 HMSO, 1988).

Parts of this chapter have appeared in articles in *New Statesman and Society* (30 June 1989) and in the *Journal of Communications* vol. 39, no. 3, 1989.

A North/South Divide?

Ron Eagle

In the North East of England hopelessness and dereliction are by-words. In its contrast with the affluent South East, it invites associations with East Germany where the grey lifestyle of the population is dramatically different from that portrayed on the West German TV channels watched each evening. You could be forgiven for supposing that its TV advertising would be a drab imitation of glossy, metropolitan attractions.

In fact the North East of England is a thriving region, currently undergoing an economic renaissance. Salaries are marginally lower than those in the South but since house prices and travelling costs are lower, people in the North East have higher levels of disposable income. The North Easterner is likely to eat out more often than the average Southerner and the percentage of those taking two annual holidays is the same as it is in the South.

The British Market Research Board (BMRB) has identified that when it comes to youth and style the North East has a greater proportion of 'style leaders' (once known as trendsetters) per head of population than any other area in the UK.[1] It was for this reason that Beecham test-marketed their prestigious range of hair preparations 'Brylcream Black' in Tyne Tees, rather than with the supposedly upmarket youth of the South.

The North East boasts the largest and third-largest shopping centres in Europe, less than five miles away from each other. Marks & Spencer's first out-of-town store was built in the Gateshead Metrocentre. Boasting 2 million square feet, and still expanding, it is twice the size of Brent Cross. Sears Holdings, the owners of Miss Selfridge, Dolcis and Olympus Sports amongst others, first housed their various businesses under one roof in Gateshead. Major retailers such as Boots and Marks & Spencer report that their North East stores are first or second in their national sales league and Newcastle was the preferred option for Hennes, the Scandinavian fashion store, when they were looking to expand out of London.

The problem is perception and misconception. While the North East might be thought of as the heartland of economic deprivation, the region's population has money to spend and more places in which to spend it. North Easterners are also more likely to buy brands than own-labels (as true in the fashion as it is in the FMCG sector[2]), and (with only a few exceptions) see the same TV commercials.

An average thirty-second TV commercial costs anything between £70,000 to £100,000 to make, so few clients indulge in regional variations. In other words, the same advertisement is shown across the country. However, advertisers are largely aware of consumption patterns and of the attitudes to products in each of the ITV regions and will weight their advertising activity accordingly. Clearly, if the product is unavailable in the North East or would only be bought in small quantities, Tyne Tees would not be offered advertising.

Viewers in the North East have seen advertisements for BMW cars, high-interest savings accounts and many other premium products. The majority of financial products and services advertise in the North East. However it is true to say that in terms of corporate advertising, and that directed specifically to, let's say, Fund Managers, Tyne Tees takes a much smaller percentage of the advertising cake than the region's 5 per cent share of the UK population would suggest.

Where differences do occur they are marginal. Fewer people in the North read a national newspaper and so this is reflected in the advertisement revenue Tyne Tees takes from this sector. Similarly, we earn less from the airline/business travel sector since most of this takes place in London and the South. The consumption of beers, ales and lagers always have distinctive regional patterns. Our advertising reflects local brews, such as Best Scotch, but a high proportion of lager consumption in the North East is in the premium priced sector.

A more loyal audience means that advertisers reach their required weights of advertising more quickly. Instead of being an incentive to spend, the converse has proved to be true. Money has been taken from the high viewing areas to bolster the flagging audiences of the South. Airtime is television's product, it must sell it all or give it away; unlike other products it can't be controlled according to market circumstances. Thus, the only true North-South divide exists in the cost of reaching a desirable market, such as housewives, adults, AB men. We believe that, after 1993, airtime will cease to be traded as a commodity and revenue will become more closely related to audience delivery.

The average North East individual watches 23 per cent more television than his or her counterpart in London and 16 per cent more when compared to the South. If we look at today's most sought-after market, the 16–24 ABC 1s (young and up-market), the same trend applies. It could be argued that as a percentage of the total North East population, we have less of this prestige demographic group than the South. However, the cost of reaching each of those in the South is up to three times the cost of reaching them on Tyne Tees.

In order to make inroads on the advertising shortfall, Tyne Tees has had to reappraise its presentation and sales methods. In a system which rewards sin and punishes virtue we have to make airtime good value for money. Tyne Tees has developed a totally integrated facility, where for a single charge we are able to provide advertising agencies with distribution in five retail sectors (grocers, off-licences, DIY, chemists and public houses), airtime to promote the brands, and a research model that tells you the brand's likely performance throughout the UK. Secondly, we have examined financial lifestyles and attitudes throughout the UK, and tracked spending habits since Royal Assent was given to the Building Societies Act and the Financial Services Act. This has given us unique information with which we can advise clients on how, and to whom, they should target their advertising.

Penetration of new services such as Channel 5, Sky and BSB will make slow but steady progress throughout the 1990s. The North East (depending on price) will probably see a faster rate of installation of these services, as witnessed by the growth of VCRs in the late 1970s and 1980s. However, I am sure that ITV will remain brand leaders to the late 1990s, and within the network of ITV companies, Tyne Tees Television will still have one of the highest per capita indices of viewing on the network.

Notes

1. BMRB, a private research organisation, supplies the Target Group Index, an annual survey based on a sample of 24,000, which asks questions about consumption of goods and related viewing habits of those using major brands.
2. Fast Moving Consumer Goods, i.e. grocery products.

A Particularly Valuable Service

Samantha Cook

'Only my generation, who grew up without radio or TV, can really appreciate its worth.' (JF, 75, retired chartered secretary, Dorset)

All quotations in this article are taken from diaries written by the over-60s for the national *One Day in the Life of Television* project, organised by the Television Unit of the British Film Institute. Invited to write diaries about their viewing on 1 November 1988, some 16,000 people responded. As well as statistical information, the diaries offer profound personal insights into how viewers feel about television and the role it plays in their lives. Because of the self-selected nature of the participants, the limitations of being restricted to one day's viewing, and the structure of the project, in which viewers were invited to respond to prompter questions, I make no definitive conclusions about the nature of the elderly as an audience, but refer to the considerable response (1,090 diaries from over-60s) to offer shade and texture to any argument about their status as a 'neglected audience'.

From the 1,090 diaries 'typical' or recurring responses were selected and quotations chosen if the opinion had been stated by over 100 people. Then, as far as possible, I have attempted to use diaries from across the range of geography, class and gender. This proved more difficult; perhaps inevitably there was a large number of middle-class respondents, and, interestingly, more women than men wrote in. Outside these criteria my choices, to a great extent, were random; and it is with regret that so many revealing and incisive comments had to be left out.

Little has been written in Britain about the importance of the elderly as television viewers. Neither BBC/BARB/IBA statistics which depend on ratings, nor advertising research, which addresses viewers only in terms of what they spend, are enough if we wish to analyse how and why people watch, and whether or not their viewing needs are supplied. In America much work has been done that is relevant to the British situation, proving the importance of the older population in terms of its sheer size, and its predominance in the total television audience.

There are 14 million people aged 55+ and 8 million aged 65+ in Britain today, and this figure is set to increase.[1] Between 1985 and 2005, due to improved health care and medical technology, and a declining birthrate, there will be an 8 per cent increase in the 60+ population (compared to a 4 per cent increase in the rest of the population) and the 55+ age group will increase by a staggering 74 per cent.[2]

Roughly 25 per cent of the country's total television viewing is done by those aged 65+, who watch on average about 50 per cent more television than the population as a whole, averaging about 37 hours per week. A third of the elderly have difficulty hearing, and one in ten wear hearing aids, which inevitably limits radio usage.[3] Since the elderly already watch more television than any other group, devoting more time to television than any other single activity except sleeping,[4] and since they are set to grow massively in number, they should be foregrounded rather than ignored in discussions on how deregulation will affect audiences. In many cases, due to a more limited mobility and lifestyle than other sectors of the population, the elderly are more 'available' to view; so, for example, on a winter's evening 95 per cent might tune in.[5]

I am 73 years of age, a retired Customs Officer living alone in rented accommodation, net income about £90.00 per week. Unless I am going out for the evening to attend a class or the occasional social visit, I have my rented TV set turned on from about 5 p.m. to midnight. I make no excuses, at least I hear a human voice.

(MD, Kent)

When I became widowed and living alone, television became very often a lifeline to the outside world. It is switched on considerably more than it used to be; sometimes not listened to at all but as a background to reading, sewing, cleaning, crosswords, decorating, letter-writing etc., etc.

(DS, 71, retired restaurateur, Cheshire)

46

Before starting this piece, I was aware of treading potentially dangerous ground by glibly referring to the elderly as if, by the nature of
their age alone, they are a homogeneous, cohesive group. A working
concept of the elderly is very slippery. In our society we do not know
how to treat the elderly as people, let alone how to use the term
considerately. The subject makes us uneasy. We all fear growing old.
We are uncomfortable and guilty about our fear and loathing, and
tend to patronise or ignore. Academic study cannot work in a
vacuum, and is therefore subject to these same tensions. How old is
elderly? 50? 55? 65? Different researchers set different limits. What
do we imply when we label an audience 'elderly'? How do these
implications affect race, gender and class? Are these to be swept aside
in the assertion that age is the most important variable? There will be
real differences in the ways in which a seventy-three year old retired
customs officer from Kent and a sixty-three year old housewife from
Northern Ireland use their television, and differences in the extent to
which they are, or will be, 'neglected'. Researching this article forced
me to face these anxieties, if not to dispel them. It is absolutely
fundamental to question our deep-rooted cultural assumptions
about what it means to be old before we study the elderly as an
audience. Why should it come as any surprise that 10% of the
audience for *Top of the Pops*, and 18% for *Blue Peter* are aged 55 or
over?[6] Why should we presume that the range and viewing interests
of older people should be narrower than those of any other age
group?

> Perhaps my choice reflects my age, but there again I also like *Top
> of the Pops*, Muriel Gray and never miss Jonathan Ross, whilst I
> long for the return of Dame Edna.
>
> (LL, 76, retired, London)

Rubin and Rubin, two American researchers, have argued that
rather than define the elderly by age alone, a new concept of ageing
might be established which is more dependent on contextual factors,
rather than on a notion of biological chronology. In this way, various
social influences (including health and mobility, economic security,
social activity, interpersonal interaction and environmental context)
are seen as the most significant variables in viewing behaviours. To
illustrate this argument, they demonstrate that the viewing habits of
a group of elderly people in an enclosed environment (not dissimilar
to a study by Nan MacLeod-Engel[7]) did not differ substantively
from those of younger people in that same environment.[8]

However problematic the concept of the elderly, it is not the only
term which we should question. Attempts should be made at least to

47

clarify just how it is assumed the elderly are neglected. Special programmes which deal with what are believed to be their needs and interests? Ranges of representations of themselves that 'reflect' reality? It is often argued that programmes aimed at an older audience are, like other 'minority' programming, shunted into 'ghetto' schedules (morning, weekends, afternoons). In the USA, Gerbner et al. argue that television doesn't represent the population truthfully, i.e. proportionally according to real age–group patterns. The vast majority of characters on American television are in the 25–60 age range, which broadcasters argue are the age groups which make up the majority of consumers. They also note that where old people are represented, they are far more likely to be foolish or eccentric characters, treated with 'disrespect' in the narrative. Old women, in particular, are more likely to be seen as 'silly' than old men, or women in other age groups. Their conclusion, which treads the dangerous ground of implying that 'they' (the audience) unlike 'we' (the researchers) believe all they see on the screen, is that heavy users of television are most likely to have negative thoughts about the elderly and about ageing.[9] Korzenny and Neuendorf, also in the United States, stress that representations of the elderly are less important in their effect on the ways in which the older population are seen than on their own self esteem. They argue that, when the elderly have little other social contact, television is an essential referent for positive self-image and thus for encouraging integration into society.[10]

While the situation in the United States sounds remarkably similar to that in Britain, if we look to the diaries it is interesting that elderly viewers do not express a sense of being neglected. Out of a representative sample (ranging through class, gender, geography, opinion) of sixty diaries, only one referred to representations, and this in a positive manner, as opposed to the thirty-three subjects who referred to their fears of deregulation, for example. MF, 64, retired, writes of Helen Daniels, the glamorous granny in *Neighbours*,

> Why can't I be like Helen? Supercook – housewife – grandmother – businesswoman – artist – driver – voluntary counsellor – gardener – organiser. She reminds me of the song Peggy Lee sings, 'I'm a Woman W.O.M.A.N.' who can do anything at the drop of a hat.

What about 'Elderly Programming'? It may be easy to argue that there are not enough programmes for the elderly. But how are we defining such a programme? As with 'youth programming', researchers, producers and programmers risk relying on very shaky assumptions. For, while it is undeniable that people of the same age will share many of the same interests, to presume that age means predominantly negative and debilitating things is not the way to win over an elderly audience. At present, programming for the elderly consists of vocational, leisure and consumer programmes, and according to the ratings it is successful. BBC Research from 1988 shows that it was the elderly (here the 55+) who made up the largest audience of the following programmes: *Years Ahead* (a magazine programme on Channel Four for retired people), 79.3 per cent; *Victorian Kitchen Garden* (a nostalgic social history programme on BBC 2), 70.7 per cent; *Fifteen to One* (fast moving quiz game on Channel Four featuring a number of elderly contestants), 70.6 per cent; *Noticeboard* (information and consumer advice, etc. on Channel Four), 68.9 per cent and *Mavis on Four* (Channel Four teatime chat show with Mavis Nicholson), 65.6 per cent.

That these five programmes are on BBC 2 or Channel Four (with its statutory obligation to provide minority programming) and are daytime programmes, underlines their marginal status in the schedule. However, if we look at programmes which are most popular amongst the 55+ (i.e. when we log how large a percentage of the available 55+ audience is watching), a very different pattern emerges. The top five programmes in this case were: *Coronation Street* (49.2 per cent); *Bergerac* (46 per cent); *After Henry* (44.2 per cent); *News at 5.45* (43 per cent) and *Sporting Triangles* (42.5 per cent). This tallies much more with the viewing habits of the rest of the population.[11]

Seen in this light, the term 'neglected' needs to be questioned. It threatens to ascribe passivity to a group of people already assumed, within our culture, to be passive. The elderly, like any other audience, bring contexts and histories to the screen, creating possibilities for producing their own meanings and pleasures over a range of programmes. To assume that positive representations or target programming is all an elderly audience wants from television is misguided.

How then, do the elderly use television? If they do not see themselves as an age group, nor as a neglected audience, this is still not to say that they have unmitigated praise for the current broadcasting system. Their relationship with television is no less complex than the rest of the population's. To some, fears about losing mental faculties can cause a tension in their enjoyment. They wish to engage with and respond to the world around them, and find that television helps them do this, yet many suffer from the common anxiety that television watching is a mind-numbing experience, inferior somehow to other more worthwhile activities. There is some guilt about 'time-wasting', watching television during the day (particularly in the case of the women), and a heightened fear (as compared to diarists of other age groups) of behaving passively or unthinkingly.

> As a general rule I never watch TV in the morning and very seldom in the afternoon. I prefer to follow my own pursuits. I have many interests. I'm still involved with playgroups, I go to keep fit, I play badminton, I read, I go to concerts and naturally shop and see my friend.
>
> (MD, 60, retired)

> I never watch TV before about 7.15 p.m. even when I am at home, as I have far more interesting things to do: most evenings when we are in, we listen to classical music on discs, tapes or the radio and only choose to watch TV when the programmes are of particular interest.
>
> (RB, 62, piano teacher, Halifax)

Many diarists would agree with WG, 75, housewife:

> I am a television fan but I have always used it for me, not letting it use me.

Probably even more than other audiences, the elderly depend on television for information and education.

> As a pensioner with severe mobility problems, I may not be a majority viewer, but I am one of a large number for whom TV is an essential part of life for many hours of the day. In no other way can I keep up-to-date with advances in the activities in which I used to be able to play an influential part, for I have to spend 18–20 hours a day in bed now. This could be rather lonely at times but for the blessing of the radio, TV and video beside me.
>
> (AB, 69, housewife, Devon)

The desire to engage with the world can take different forms: enjoying quiz shows for example, especially in the case of *Fifteen to One* (Channel Four).

> Tuesday afternoon I visit a lady I used to work with, and we always watch *Fifteen to One*. We look forward to it for it helps keep our minds active seeing what we can answer.
>
> (HT, 63, housewife, Nottinghamshire)

> Watch *Fifteen to One*, as always – sometimes get answers right

50

myself, and it doesn't consist exclusively of 'bubbly' photogenics picked for similar programmes – the fat and old get a chance to show their brains, bless them (and their wise producer).

(TS, 66, retired secretary, Surrey)

4–4.30 p.m. *Fifteen to One* Ch. 4. A dully presented quiz, which is good for my ego. I always feel more confident that I am keeping senility at bay when I know most of the answers.

(MD, retired customs officer, Kent)

Teletext information services also seem to be very important, as are the news programmes, and documentaries.

As I am an octogenarian and can no longer read as much as I would like, I find the television news and current affairs programmes a good way of keeping up-to-date and a particularly valuable service.

(EA, 85, retired, Basingstoke)

But it's all the lovely documentaries I really enjoy: *40 Minutes, Out of the Doll's House,* lots of lovely cookery programmes, the wondrous gardening programmes, antique shows, other people's houses, other people's hobbies, passions – other people! Architecture, politics (not party), philosophy, the whole wide world in the living room, from the beginning of time to right now. A succession of talking heads, looking right at me; royals, medics, comics, criminals – would that my friends were as diverting.

(SR, 61, Kent)

Even more than education and information, television is very important to alleviate the loneliness of the isolated elderly. As well as offering company, and a persona to which to respond, it can broaden otherwise limited experiences, and its importance as a conversation piece is perhaps more resonant than for other age groups.

The glory of television at its best enables the viewer to get the measure of a personality whom one would otherwise never encounter and who, no doubt, in 'real' life one would have precious little in common with. It thus extends the breadth of one's human sympathy (I recall being very impressed by a man who was very big in pigs in a remote tribe in New Guinea).

(RT, 66, parish clerk, Surrey)

Finally, even accounting for the anxiety about too much tele-

51

vision-watching that runs through many of the diaries, its function as entertainment cannot be underrated. However, the following quotations show just how diverse notions of entertainment can be; and how important an idea of quality is to many elderly viewers.

I particularly like the well-made dramatisations of novels: for example *The Mayor of Casterbridge*, *Brideshead Revisited*, any Dickens or Trollope.

(LS, 71, retired, Manchester)

The invasion of chat shows – situation comedies, phone-ins and breakfast TV etc. came from America and its citing as 'entertainment' is in doubt.

(AS, 70, retired, Huddersfield).

I am grateful for the chance, when it comes, to see some of the best classical plays, operas and some ballet. I do dislike it, though, when people introducing the programmes, on TV or in the magazines, will tell us kindly that we needn't be afraid of Shakespeare, Wagner and whoever, because really they were ordinary people just like us and wrote plays and music about ordinary people just like us. Someone the other day started telling me that opera wasn't just for rich people. So I turned him off. Does he think only the boxes and dress circles are filled in the theatres?

(JB, 71, retired domestic worker, Darlington)

The term 'quality' is much-used in the diaries. While it is tempting to contest the commonsense way in which diarists use the word (begging the questions: who defines 'quality television'?, who makes it? who is it for?), it is essential to understand that audiences do see it in straightforward terms of 'good' television, and that it is a key term in understanding the overwhelmingly negative responses to deregulation. These responses are articulated less from a conservative fear of change or the future (most diarists were adventurous viewers, unafraid to be critical of television today) than from a real concern about the predicted decline in programme standards when producers will have to compete for the largest audiences. However exaggerated some of the terminology ('trash', etc.) used to describe commercial television, it is nevertheless telling to discover that these are the terms in which many viewers comprehend the future.

I think I can recognise 'quality' when I see it, and equally, I know 'rubbish' when I see it! So can thousands and thousands of others.

(WS, 64, retired manager, Belfast)

Having just returned from a holiday in Canada, I do not view the prospect of multichannel TV with any enthusiasm at all, I fear that we may descend to the same low standards as those in Canada and the USA. It would be a great loss if there were no more programmes about music, opera, ballet, travel, the countryside and architecture for those are the ones I enjoy the most. Time will tell.

(HL, 60, housewife, Merseyside).

Supposing pay-as-you-go TV comes in? I'll only ever pay for the things I know I like, and I'll never learn anything new. Miss all the marvellous education progs, and progs for training dogs, and progs for the deaf. Perhaps I'd be too mean to have a TV at all, and then I might write a book, or take up painting.

(SR, 61, Kent)

The argument that deregulation will offer more choice is obviously much contested by elderly viewers. Even if the rise of cable, video and direct broadcast satellite increases the number of programmes for viewers to select, that choice will not be open to all. Many will be excluded by economic necessity. Will the majority of elderly viewers be able to afford satellite dishes, cable and subscription fees? Many are surviving today on subsistence pensions. Elderly households are already less likely to be provided with amenities and consumer durables than other households.[12] The expense of keeping a television was brought up in many diaries; in some more seriously than others.

If the cost of having TV continues and quality drops further, I shall have to give up. Cost approximately £5.00. a week altogether – take that out of a 'basic pension'!

(WH, 77, retired, York)

I wish I could stand up in the House of Commons and ask one or two members of Parliament to come home with me for one month and see how we try to survive. It's nearly impossible, what with standing charges on gas, electricity, telephone plus VAT before you even use anything; also TV licences – now the poll tax coming on, now the £10 for glasses and teeth which Mrs Thatcher says is only a small amount, but changes her mind when we get an extra £10 at Xmas – it then becomes a big amount: the cold weather must make it increase, I suppose.

(RH, 68, retired cook, Middlesex)

As far as I can see, cable television will be far too expensive for me to install, and in any case, if all it will amount to is twenty or thirty

times the sort of drivel we are suffering at the moment, or worse –
scrub it!! I'm not interested! ... I don't know about putting up
licence fees. I think we are all due a massive refund for putting up
with *Emmerdale Farm*.

(WL, 66, retired, Leeds)

These are audiences who will not be able to afford to have information services, no matter how useful they are for anyone who uses
their television to learn about the world. The wonders of electronic
banking and remote control shopping may well be out of the reach of
the very people who could make productive use of them: the house-
bound, ill or isolated, amongst whom the elderly predominate, and
those who cannot afford cable or satellite will be left with a destabilised terrestrial broadcasting system, limited by the onslaught of
commercial competition.

What of those older people who will be able to afford cable and
satellite? Advertiser Alasdair Ritchie argues that a large proportion
of the over-50s (advertisers, it would seem, regard anyone above 50
as elderly) are big savers, willing to spend on consumer durables.[13]
Other evidence suggests that some sectors of the elderly are financially more secure than much of the younger population. For example, in 1985, 46 per cent of the population aged over 65 owned their
own property, as compared to only 15 per cent of those under 65.[14]
Ritchie argues that as one-third of the population is over 50, with
£108 billion per year to spend, and as they are adventurous but wise
spenders, their importance as consumers should not be undervalued.
We have now seen how negatively most older viewers look upon
deregulation, but with money to spend on the receiver and the
subscription fees, leisure time in which to select from the expanded
number of channels available, and a lifestyle improved with remote
control shopping and home information services, the wealthier
elderly are an ideal target audience, in an ideology that defines an
audience by its power to spend and where 'choice' marks the capacity to consume. Securing essential services should not be left to
spending power.

It is not, however, my intention to argue that deregulation will be
positive for some of the elderly because it might broaden their
consumer choices. This argument loses much of its strength anyway
when we see the light in which older viewers hold advertising:

TV-am is interrupted, just as it gets interesting, by advertising
breaks, which usually annoy me as they are for toys that always
seem to cost practically the whole week's old age pension.

(MCH, 73, retired, Sussex)

And I don't watch advertisements. Most of them are an insult to normal intelligence. When I hear of millions, even billions of pounds being spent annually on advertisements I wonder how that affects the price and quality of the product.

(JB, 71, retired domestic worker, Darlington)

Channel Four ads, slots for which seem to be unduly concentrated in the News, have an anthropological charm for one who retired from the rat race eight years ago. In one tonight a yuppie stereo-type, who owns a pocket computer, is the Jones the punters are meant to keep up with and his envious companion loads himself progressively with the gear the computer is supposed to replace. Can anyone actually buy such a gadget after watching such humourless garbage or do the ad men know only too well what will ring the bell?

(RT, 66, parish clerk, Surrey)

Consumer choices are not what elderly viewers are demanding. It is other choices that matter.

It is suggested that the competition for viewers may lead to less, not more, real choice. In any case, is it desirable that we should all be watching TV non-stop?

(LS, 71, retired, Manchester)

I fear the coming choice of the cable and satellite age. Will the boom of TV self-destruct with too many alternatives? My hope will be that the dictionary definition of 'choice' – the preferable or best part and worthy of being chosen – will ultimately prevail for the benefit of all people everywhere.

(AL, 61, retired, Scotland)

In an ideal world, the possibility of expanding choices would mean broadcasting a range of programme styles and content to meet the multifarious needs of different audiences. To neglect the wide-ranging interests of an audience as large and fast growing as the elderly could be disastrous. If deregulated competition means fear of experiment and a withering of 'quality', it may be the audiences themselves who do the neglecting. Producers and planners should remember that, in the words of MC (69, retired, from Suffolk), 'We don't lose our marbles when we get old...'

Notes

1. Andrew Hemming, *Elderly People's Use of Broadcast Media* (BBC, 1988).
2. OPCS, *General Household Survey 1986* (HMSO, 1989).
3. Ibid.
4. Irene Shaw, *Elderly People's Use of the Media* (BBC, 1982).
5. Hemming, *Elderly People's Use of Broadcast Media.*
6. Ibid.
7. *The Role of Television in The Daily Lives of the Elderly* was presented to the International Television Studies Conference in London in 1986. Macleod-Engel draws useful conclusions: that television can act as an orientation function for the elderly; for information or education; or for entertainment; or for escapism, or even as a mechanism to exert power over other viewers in the same room. However, her study is somewhat limited by the size of her sample: eight 'key' informants, two 'confused' informants, all men, who are confined to an institution.
8. A. M. Rubin and R. B. Rubin, 'Age, Context and Television Use', *Journal of Broadcasting* vol. 25, no. 1, 1981.
9. G. Berbner, L. Gross, N. Signorielli and M. Morgan, 'Ageing with Television: Images on Television Drama and Conceptions of Social Reality', *Journal of Communication* vol. 30, no. 1, 1980.
10. F. Korzenny and K. Neuendorf, 'Television Viewing and Self Concept of the Elderly', *Journal of Communication* vol. 30, no. 1, 1980.
11. Hemming, *Elderly People's Use of Broadcast Media.*
12. OPCS, *General Household Survey.*
13. Alasdair Ritchie, 'Open View: Tacking a £108,000,000,000 Market', *LWT Marketing Review* Issue 80, April 1989. See also his article on pp. 57–60 of this volume.
14. OPCS, *General Household Survey.*

Mature Markets

Alasdair Ritchie

'Over the hill', 'fuddy duddy', 'of no importance to us marketeers'. These are just some of the conventional expressions used about old people by many people in advertising and marketing. They could not be further from the truth.

In a survey on the over-50s market, initiated by Holmes Knight Ritchie/wRG during the autumn of 1987, some interesting facts emerged. The over-50s now constitute one-third of the entire population in Britain, and (as Chart 1 shows) it is the only age group which will grow into the next century. Longevity means that there are fewer widows and more couples, and that the wealth created (often from inherited parental property) has seen the emergence of the 'vocational pensioner'. Labels ascribed to this age group ('guppies', 'wrinklies', 'crinklies') were firmly rejected, and the survey revealed that this age group is much more adventurous and free-spirited than younger people believe. With fewer financial commitments such as mortgages or families, the over-50s have more money to spend on themselves than any other age group – £108 billion a year. And they *do* spend. Chart 2 illustrates how pensioners' share of spending has, over the last 15 years, moved from the essentials of food and energy to luxuries. They are also discriminating in what they buy. They are, after all, the 'Hoover' generation when things were built to last, so they look for quality products that are well made and good value for money. They see through hype and abhor brash sales talk.

Some of this background information is important to an understanding of how the older age group view television. Although some of the 'old favourites' are predictable, their viewing is eclectic. However, programmes which have particular appeal would seem to contain at least some of the following elements:

- a strong, preferably uncomplicated storyline;
- human interest and emotion;
- nostalgia;
- current affairs;
- studio shows;
- viewer participation;
- humour.

CHART 1

POPULATION FORECAST BY AGE GROUP 1985 - 2015

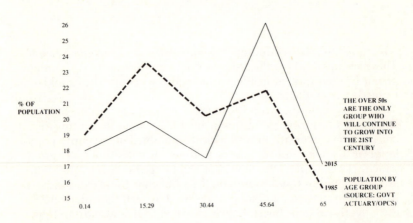

THE OVER 50s ARE THE ONLY GROUP WHO WILL CONTINUE TO GROW INTO THE 21ST CENTURY

POPULATION BY AGE GROUP (SOURCE: GOVT ACTUARY/OPCS)

CHART 2

AVERAGE ANNUAL % REAL GROWTH PENSIONERS SPENDING 1970 - 1985

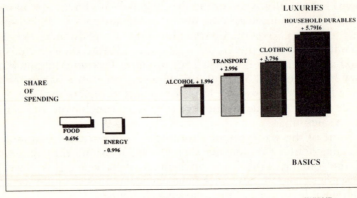

LUXURIES

HOUSEHOLD DURABLES + 5.79%

CLOTHING + 3.79%

TRANSPORT + 2.99%

ALCOHOL + 1.99%

SHARE OF SPENDING

FOOD -0.69%

ENERGY - 0.99%

BASICS

(SOURCE: FES)

INCOME

58

The programmes which seemed to have the most appeal (between 3 April and 2 July 1989) were *Coronation Street, Busman's Holiday, Emmerdale Farm, News at Ten, Tanamera, News at 5.40 p.m., This is Your Life*, on ITV; and *Treasure Hunt; 15–1*, and *Countdown* on Channel Four.

As people get older they tend to watch television more, although 'upmarket' adults watch less than their 'mass market' contemporaries. However, older viewers of all classes watch more television than younger people. The HKR survey showed that over-50s did not think TV programmes were 'as good as they used to be' (even though they watch relatively more), and protested this was not a matter of wearing rose-coloured spectacles. It is clear that this age group forms a critical television audience and appreciates a good yarn and a good laugh.

Channel Four, supposedly the channel for younger viewers, compares well to ITV among the over-55s during the day time. This has a lot to do with programming, as the TVR figures from 16.00 on ITV and Channel 4 in July 1988 show. A TVR is an audience measurement figure. The nearer to zero it is, the fewer people are viewing; the nearer 20 or 30, the more people are viewing. The two quarter-hours from 16.30 on ITV (a weekday average) achieved 3 and 4 TVR. On Channel Four however, 12 TVR for the over-55s were achieved for each quarter. Channel Four not only provides more absolute ratings, but when re-applied to the more prosperous ABC 1 sector the proportion makes impressive reading. So *Countdown*, another Channel Four programme, will typically get a TVR of 8 with all adults, but double that with the over-55s.

HKR/WRG Ltd produced and developed a TV campaign for Saga Holidays, aimed especially at the over-55s. The objective was to obtain the highest possible conversion factors from all adult TV viewers to the over-55s, so TV advertising was used selectively in order to reach this target group most cost-effectively. 'Conversion factors' is advertising industry terminology: when looking at conversion factors you are actually looking at indices. For example, *Coronation Street* may deliver a TVR of 40 adults, but it may also deliver a TVR of 56 adults of 55+, therefore achieving a conversion factor of 140 per cent (index). This means, quite simply, that a higher proportion of adults aged 55 or more are viewing this programme. The importance of this to TV advertisers is that when selecting any target group the campaign can be made more effective by selecting airtime in the appropriate programmes. The higher the conversion factor (index) achieved, the more effective this selection of airtime has been and this, hopefully, increases the chance of selling the product or service.

TV research supplied by AGB (Audits of Great Britain) highlighted various timebands across the week (coffee-time, daytime and early evening), and across both ITV and Channel Four, as the most popular viewing times for this target audience. The research also highlighted certain programmes as achieving high conversion factors in this group, and delivering the highest TVRs: the *News* on ITV at 17.40, *15–1* on Channel Four and *Coronation Street*. The normal conversion factor is 146 per cent, but by using this research data HKR/WRG achieved higher figures and targeted this specific audience group more cost-effectively: 150 per cent in Central Scotland and 153 per cent in the TSW (Television South West) region in October 1988.

So, to reach the lucrative, demanding, 'mature individualists', commercial and BBC television will have to concentrate on what people of this age group watch and tailor programmes with them more specifically in mind. Once you've got them, they're a loyal and attentive audience.

Do They Think We're Uloo?*

Ashwani Sharma

We are sitting around the TV, a typical Sunday evening ritual. Mum's writing a letter to her sister in India. My brother Sanjay is sprawled on the floor reading the *Weekend Guardian*. Sangeeta my fiancée is on the phone talking to her Grandma. I'm day-dreaming, remote control in hand. Dad walks in with the tea.

'What's on the tele?' he asks in Urdu.
    Mum replies in Punjabi, 'We're waiting for *Network East*.'
    'Yeah, at half past midnight,' brother interrupts. 'They're always putting on our programmes in the middle of the night. Ghetto programming for us ghetto people, eh?'
    I switch channels, Cagney's arresting a pimp.
    'Oh good, let's watch this.'
    'But Mum it started ages ago.'
    'It doesn't matter, it's better than that *Last Night at the Proms* rubbish,' she retorts.

So once again we watch an American import. American television dominates our family viewing. Programmes such as *Hill Street Blues*, *Cagney and Lacey*, *Dynasty*, *M*A*S*H*, and *Cosby Show* are enjoyed as 'pure entertainment' because they bear no relation to our life. Dad feels the problem with many British programmes is their 'Britishness'. As Asians we are excluded by their language, stories, humour and subject matter. With American products these factors are not important, because we do not expect to be addressed.

---

* Uloo is Hindi for 'owls'. It also can mean 'fools'.

61

Cagney and Lacey finishes. 'Switch it over,' Dad says, 'the news has started, I want to see the results of the Indian State Elections.'

'All right then.'

'Oh God, not him again . . .'

Geoffrey Howe is explaining how *we* couldn't live with an influx of three million Hong Kong Asians into *our* country.

'It's always the same, these news programmes seem to think we don't exist, remember the coverage of the 1985 "riots" here.'

Mum interrupts, 'I don't remember having seen so many white people at the same time in Handsworth. They brought in all these experts to explain this, that and the other, but as usual they ignored us.'

'They did show the documentary *Handsworth Songs*,' I say, 'that was made by a Black film group. It tried to explore the deeper themes of immigration, community and notions of Britishness.'

'Oh that's what it was,' Dad exclaims, 'I thought it was a level three programme for the Open University. These trendy Channel Four programmes are only for you so-called intellectuals who do Media Studies, read books no one can understand and watch arty foreign films.'

'OK, OK, but at least they showed it,' I reply defensively. 'Have they said anything about India yet?'

'You'll be lucky, it's only mentioned when there's a flood or a famine, or when the Queen's there. They don't seem to realise that we might be interested in events outside Britain or Europe. Many of us British people do have close ties with other parts of the world,' says Sanjay, in a patronising tone to the news presenter.

' . . . the cat was rescued by fireman before the fire could . . .'

'Nothing! I don't know why we bother.'

Of course there are some choices. The black current affairs programmes offer us alternative sources of information. In the 80s, *Eastern Eye*, *Bandung File*, *Network East*, *Here and Now* and *Ebony* have all been watched with great enthusiasm and expectation by the whole family, but we've often been disappointed; the limited airtime available has meant them addressing a number of diverse subjects in very little depth.

'How long before *Network East* starts?' Mum asks.

'Ages yet. They'll probably have the Indian state elections, East-West fashions, Islamic girls' schools, a pop group and two Indian filmclips all in a half-hour slot!'

'But at least we have some programmes made for us,' Dad cuts in. 'During the 50s and 60s there wasn't anything. I think the first one was in the early 70s. It was called *Apna Gher Sumjeye* meaning "Feel at Home". With a name like that you can guess it was really patronising.'

'The first one I remember was *Nai Zindagi Nai Jivan*,' I recall.

' "New Life, New Way", would you believe! I'd been here 20 years by then!' exclaims Dad.

'Yeah, I remember that. It was presented by a couple of austere dark-suited men speaking "BBC Urdu", and they always had heavy Indian classical music on every week. Not much good if you can't understand Urdu and are into Bhangra!' remarks Sanjay sarcastically.

Channel Four has undoubtedly had a significant effect on the viewing habits of many black families. Its commitment to innovative programming and 'minority audiences' was greeted with great interest in our home. The showing of mainstream Indian films in 1983 was a symbolic event in the lives of many South Asians. Even though many of us had seen the films before, it marked for us the broadcasting establishment's overdue recognition of the Bombay film industry and its importance to the cultural life of many families in Britain. This has been confirmed by the popularity of the series *Movie Mahal*. Mum and Dad particularly enjoyed its celebration of the Indian film industry. A major factor has been the use of Hindi as its main language.

Sangeeta finishes her phone call.

'Grandma's fine. She wanted to watch the snooker.'

'Snooker! I thought she didn't watch much TV.'

'She doesn't really, but she likes the game and it doesn't matter that she doesn't understand English. She also has the TV on for company when no one's in the house. But most of the time she watches Indian films on video.'

'It's the same with us now,' Mum says. 'We seem to be watching less and less TV and more Indian videos. Even Channel Four hasn't been showing anything new, just repeats of films and *Movie Mahal*.'

'Well there've been some black series like *Tandoori Nights* and *Desmond's*,' I remark.

'I quite liked *Tandoori Nights*,' says Mum. 'But only because it was Asian; some of it wasn't very funny though.'

'Even the BBC has jumped on Channel Four's "multi-cultural" bandwagon,' my brother remarks.

'You mean like *Sholom Salaam*,' laughs Sangeeta.

'That terrible series about a Muslim-Jewish romance?' Dad asks.

'It wasn't that bad,' defends Mum in Punjabi.

'Some of it was totally ridiculous!'

'But we all watched it, everyone I know watched it!' Sangeeta adds. 'I could identify some of the time with the Asian characters, even though I agree the story was pretty daft. But what can you expect from a white writer. At least it had strong Asian females; we don't see that often.'

'I liked *South of the Border* better, it also had a strong black female character. Makes a change from their usual prostitute roles,' my brother comments.

'They're very few positive black characters, male or female for us to identify with.'

'There's always Lenny Henry.'

'Why haven't there been any Asian comedians on TV?' Dad asks.

Nobody can answer this. The conversation continues on the theme of comedy. Mum and Dad find most of the comedy shows uninteresting, again language being the problem. 'At least things have changed, slightly. Remember only a few years ago those really offensive racist programmes such as *Mind your Language*.'

'And *It Ain't Half Hot Mum*.'

'And we used to watch them!' We all laugh, embarrassed at ourselves.

We have over the years resorted to watching some very bad television. This has meant viewing programmes which have on many occasions been insulting to us. Take for example the spate of serials set around the time of the British Empire in India. We watched with some intrigue and amusement the banal adventures of the colonialists during 'the last days of the Raj'. *Jewel In The Crown* was only watched with real interest because one of our relatives in India had a walk-on part in it! Our identification is with the Asian characters and environment, and not with the main white stars: a form of oppositional reading. This seems to be true of a lot of TV drama: we watch either with an alternative perspective or from a detached distance. Television is not socially integrated into our daily lives, it is more of an entertaining intruder which we allow in from time to time. We rarely relate to the stories and characters. Occasionally, however, a programme can generate great interest. For instance, the showing of the Indian production about partition, *Tamas*, was a very emotional experience for my parents since they had actually lived through many of the events depicted.

'I've just been reading in the paper about satellite TV: "it will offer the consumer more choice",' quotes Sanjay.

'Who said that?' asks Dad. 'Murdoch probably. What does he know about us and what we would like to watch?'

Mum cuts in, 'All we'll get is a choice of cheap, boring game shows, except they'll be in Spanish or Italian.'

'European dross instead of British, not much of an improvement!'

'Maybe the cable stations will be more interesting; they're going to be locally based as opposed to the expensive international satellite stations,' I suggest.

'But they're still going to be about making money. You'll have rich black business men trying to sell Tilda rice to us every few minutes!' Dad cynically comments.

'That isn't community television, what you need is more TV in which we can have a say, where some of the programmes are in our languages.'

'You're wasting your breath,' Mum retorts. 'Nobody's going to listen to us, they never have and never will. Nothing will change, in fact it'll probably get worse.'

'Hey, *Network East* has started at least.'

' . . . and for the main feature, we'll be meeting the Leicester-based fashion student who's integrating Asian fabrics with Western styles.'

We look at each other in frustration.

'Let's watch an Indian video instead.'

I would like to acknowledge the help I received from Sanjay Sharma and Sangeeta Patel in writing this chapter.

Beyond Negative or Positive Images

Thérèse Daniels

The discussion surrounding the televisual depiction of black people and race relations in Britain has been bitter. There has been a great deal of dissatisfaction, expressed by Afro-Caribbean and Asian viewers, sympathetic media practitioners and academic analysts, about the portrayal of black people and the lack of programmes for black audiences.[1] In general the debate has become dominated by the twin themes of 'stereotyping' and 'negative images', to the extent that there is a marked absence of the diverse viewpoints and the general debate which surrounds television's treatment of other subjects, such as sexual relations. In this chapter I aim to show how the dominance of these critical themes has effaced a history of more varied and complex representations on British television.

The criticisms of black representation have fallen into two main areas. Firstly, there is the complaint about infrequent appearances of 'non-white' characters. A study published by the Commission for Racial Equality in 1982 showed that 'non-white' faces would appear on television screens some 10 per cent of the time.[2] These appearances would include, however, news and documentary programmes which covered foreign affairs, and American productions, which are subject to a quota of black representation. Domestic programmes, ranging from news to comedy, drama, soap opera and arts, showed hardly anything of the black British population. The study claimed, therefore, that the image television provided of Britain was of an almost all-white society. Where black people did appear, outside of the roles of deviant or entertainer, they were hardly ever in leading parts and rarely spoke. This was problematic it was said because white people were not being given the chance to get used to the idea of blacks as ordinary people. Even in the race relations dramas and comedies, such as *Love Thy Neighbour* where blacks were in leading roles, although they might be shown to be respectable and hard-working, they were still conceived as problems for the whites who had to live and work with them.

The second main criticism of television has been that where black people do appear, they tend to be in certain limited roles which are consistent with the racist stereotypes with which they are associated. The Commission for Racial Equality study found that blacks on television would often be doing menial jobs such as bus conductors, street cleaners, hospital ancillaries or factory workers. These images were said to reinforce the popular belief that blacks form a lower order of human being than whites. In many programmes blacks appeared singing and dancing, displaying their 'natural rhythm'. Afro-Caribbeans also frequently featured in a world of criminality and prostitution. Both Afro-Caribbeans and Asians, it was argued, were shown to be simple-minded, ignorant, slow-witted, uncouth and sometimes aggressive. It was argued that the accumulation of these images reinforced beliefs about the innate superiority of white people, and thus contributed towards racial disadvantage. They also helped to maintain the dislike and distrust which resulted in bad relationships between blacks and whites.

This kind of argument has been an enduring factor in the debate concerning race and television. There has, however, not been a uniform treatment of black people and race relations throughout television's history. The representations on television of black people have been more complex than the problem-oriented discourse or caricature that is often discussed. There is a great deal of interesting historical work being done, which, in common with other work which examines the black presence in Britain, would show a broader contribution by black people to British life than is generally acknowledged.[3] There have been distinct patterns to that coverage or portrayal, which can be linked to the wider circumstances of the general character of British television, and to Britain's domestic and foreign politics.

For example, on the very first television programme ever broadcast, *Variety* (BBC 1936), appeared Buck and Bubbles, American stars of the Cotton club. They were described in the *Radio Times* as 'versatile comedians who dance, play the piano, sing and cross-chat'. They were, of course, a variety act, and throughout the early years of television black people appeared mainly on variety and music programmes. This is perhaps unsurprising, as there has always been a place for black singers and dancers in British and American popular entertainment, despite the often deeply racist context in which artists have been forced to work. However, it must be borne in mind that initially there were very few hours of television and relatively few

67

programme formats: there were no television soap operas in the 30s and 40s for example. The focus of attention for British broadcasting in the 30s and 40s was still radio.

Black people did occasionally appear in other areas, such as plays and travelogues, but only very infrequently. In the 1950s, however, there was a broadening of representation, mainly in the area of current affairs. The burgeoning in this field was directly linked to Britain's political situation at home and abroad. There were programmes on both channels which looked at the social, political and economic conditions abroad, in Britain's colonies and elsewhere. The issue of decolonisation featured strongly. There was much fascination with India during and after its independence from a long period of British rule. Ghana was the first West African colony to achieve independence, in 1957, and several programmes suggested that its process of independence would be seen as a model for other African countries to follow. The long-running series *Commonwealth Magazine* (BBC) focused on cultural and human interest stories, as well as on the politics of the various Commonwealth countries. There were other programmes on these themes such as *International Commentary* and *Meet the Commonwealth* (both BBC).

Television also began a tentative look at the domestic situation of race relations. There were documentary programmes which looked at the issue of a colour bar, or at 'mixed marriages'. There were plays which attempted to understand the difficulties which black people were facing in Britain, such as the BBC drama-documentary *A Man from the Sun* (1956). This play featured Cy Grant, who, along with a number of other artists such as Winifred Atwell, Elizabeth Welch, Shirley Bassey and Cleo Laine, made regular and frequent appearances on television, albeit mainly as singers, although Welch and Grant were also actors. By the late 1950s Cy Grant had become a television celebrity, appearing on the *Tonight* programme as well as on daytime women's programmes such as *Leisure and Pleasure* and *For Women* (all BBC). Black American stars were also held in esteem. Paul Robeson appeared on *Sunday Night at the London Palladium* (Associated Rediffusion) and in his own specials. In 1958 Harry Belafonte appeared in his own BBC programme on Christmas Day, had his picture on the cover of the *Radio Times* and was featured inside.

It is, of course, true that the appearance of black entertainers is not in itself evidence of an enlightened attitude by either programme planners or viewers, but this was not the only area in which they featured. There was, from time to time, discussion of political leaders past and present, interviews with the wives of Indian Ambassadors on women's programmes for example, programmes on world religions, Indian films and art. There was also, throughout the fifties, a series called *Asian Club* (BBC), in which Asians (in the wider sense in which the term was then used) would hold studio discussions to which they would invite speakers from a wide range of activities. Neither the speakers nor the topics needed to be related in any obvious way to Asia. Famous or knowledgeable people would be called upon to discuss any subject of interest, from scientific research to life after death. This seems startlingly progressive given the struggles which it took to get more narrowly focused programmes on the air in the 1980s for Afro-Caribbean and Asian audiences.

There were differences between the two channels' uses of black images. The BBC had far more educational and documentary features than the ITV channels, which had more music and variety shows, and also more jungle-based drama series, such as *Ramar of the Jungle*, *Jungle Jim* and *White Hunter*, where the lead characters were white. This is related to the differences in ethos which governed the two networks. It seems that the BBC, with its strong emphasis on education and enlightenment, took the role of helping to lead public opinion on race, rather than pandering to it. The descriptions in the *Radio Times* of many of their documentary programmes suggest an anxiety to ensure that Britain's post-war and post-imperial domestic race relations should be harmonious, and that in no way should they be like those of the United States of America.

These early programmes were not, on the whole, designed with a conception of a black audience in mind. With the exception of *Asian Club*, they were created in an attempt to help the white British understand the blacks at home and abroad. During the late 1960s and the 70s, programmes such as *Till Death Us Do Part* (BBC 1966–74) and *Love Thy Neighbour* (Thames Television 1972–1975) were introduced, and were accused of using racism to increase the viewing figures. *The Fosters* (London Weekend Television 1976–77) was an attempt to show a black family as ordinary and unexceptional, with a recognition that black people might enjoy watching such a programme. Black people also appeared in soap operas; fleetingly in *Coronation Street* and more regularly in *Crossroads*. In general, however, there were no programmes for black audiences, with two exceptions. One was *Empire Road* (BBC 1978–79), a drama serial with an Afro-Caribbean and an Asian family at its centre, which was conceived with a black audience in mind, but had only two short series. The other was *Nai Zindage Naya Jeevan*, broadcast from 1965 from the BBC's education unit for Asian viewers. This was, until 1982, the only national programme for an ethnic minority audience.

Channel Four began broadcasting in 1982, and was given a specific brief to cater for minority views and tastes, including those of the ethnic minorities. Channel Four decided, in common with the approach adopted in education and local government during the 80s, that there were two significant cultural groups which should be provided for, each with different interests and concerns. To this end it commissioned London Weekend Television to make *Black on Black* and *Eastern Eye* for Afro-Caribbeans and Asians respectively. There was clearly a challenge, implicit in the new channel's innovative approach, to the BBC to match some of its more interesting initiatives. With a programme already existing for Asians, it was decided to have another for Afro-Caribbeans, *Ebony*.

Black on Black and *Eastern Eye* received some bitter criticism during their three-year runs on the grounds that they lacked guts, and merely offered a package tour for white viewers of black cultures. Much of the criticism came as a result of the dashed hope that, with Channel Four's commissioning structure and commitment to the independent sector, an independent black group would be given responsibility for such a series. No such expectations had been building up about the BBC's programme, which has consequently received less attention, and less criticism, than the other two.

Black on Black and *Eastern Eye* were replaced in 1985 with *Bandung File*, a documentary-style programme made by an independent production company, Bandung Productions, headed by Darcus Howe and Tariq Ali. This programme has a longer slot, and is on earlier, than were the other two. It treats the African, Caribbean and Asian populations as one political entity with similar concerns, although individual stories may focus on one section of the community. The items are dealt with in greater depth than they were on *Black on Black* and *Eastern Eye* and there is far greater coverage of international affairs than on *Ebony*. *Bandung File* also has the scope for a more explicitly political stance than the BBC's programme, since Channel Four's remit is differently worded from that of the BBC. *Ebony* appears to be supplementing its magazine format with in-depth documentaries, probably in response to the praise which has greeted *Bandung File*'s more serious treatment of issues. *Nai Zindage Naya Jeevan* was replaced in 1987 with *Network East*, a magazine programme in the style of *Ebony*, with a wholly English language presentation.

There have been, during the late 1980s, many more appearances of black people on British television across the range of programmes.[4] Some programme-makers appear to be using black images to demonstrate a realist, up-to-date attitude to their subjects. However, the debate on stereotyping continues to dominate discussion of this issue. It is not possible to say with any certainty whether this trend will continue, and whether deregulation will increase or reduce the opportunities for black performers and writers to get their work on screen. However, the small but growing interest in black creative work should allow practitioners to push back the boundaries of black representation beyond the single task of creating positive images. Unfortunately, at times, the opposite has been the case. Some work which has attempted to be contentious has been refused a second screening.[5] There is a possibility that rather than opening up opportunities for a wide range of dramatic portrayal, the only work that will receive an airing will be that which depicts the moral, upright, authoritative, successful black person. Whilst in the short term this would be an improvement, in the long term it will act as a constraint for writers and performers.

What lies at the heart of calls for positive images is the desire for black people to be reported, created, discussed, interpreted and criticised in a manner which recognises their essential humanity, rather than their being portrayed as symbols. Symbolism is, after all, part of the racial stereotyping through which black people have so far been understood. The challenge is for television programmes to recognise the constantly changing political factors which make race a reality, whilst attempting to challenge and transcend them.

Notes

1. See, for example, P. Cohen and C. Gardener, *It Ain't Half Racist Mum: Fighting Racism In the Media* (London: Comedia, 1982): M. Wadsworth, 'Racism In Broadcasting', in J. Curran (ed.) *Bending Reality: The State of the Media* (London: Pluto Press 1986).
2. Commission for Racial Equality, *Television in a Multi-Racial Society* (1982).
3. See P. Fryer, *Staying Power: The History of Black People in Britain* (London: Pluto Press, 1984), and 'Race and Ethnicity in British Television History', a research project in progress at the BFI Television and Projects Unit.
4. As in, currently, *Desmond's* (Channel 4); *Casualty* (BBC 1); *Capital City* (ITV); *London's Burning* (ITV); *Birds of a Feather* (BBC 1) and others.
5. The BBC, in 1986, showed *King of the Ghetto*, written by Farrukh Dhondy, on BBC 2, with a view to repeating it. Because of the offence caused to some viewers, however, this will not happen.

A Question of Image

Werbayne McIntyre

In order to assess why advertisers largely have failed to address the black population in the UK it is important to examine the ideas which decision-makers have of black people, and how these ideas are informed. In my experience quite a number of decisions are made on false assumptions caused by a number of factors, some of which I will attempt to highlight.

The ways in which demographic variables are measured produce no valid information about black people. No two sources seem to agree on just how many black people are resident in the UK and estimates range from 2.5 million to 4.5 million. The survey that should be the most accurate, the 1981 census, only numbers black people by birthplace of head of household, which is obviously inaccurate. Most other surveys are probability samples or quota samples. No one can accurately tell how many Asian or West Indian ABC 1s are resident in the UK, or what percentage of black people are car-owners. Furthermore, for the best reasons in the world, research has often been carried out in order to show that the black population is disadvantaged and therefore needs support. Headlines in the press often read that black people are disadvantaged in the jobs market, but can you recall one which said that some Asian groups were above-average buyers of Mercedes? I would suggest that negative images often go unchallenged and are assumed to be correct.

Clients of ours came to us with the assumption that if they were to recruit more West Indian and Asian staff they would have to lower the basic recruitment requirements for candidates to have 4 or 5 O Levels. When we looked at what statistics were available, most showed that the black population were proportionally better qualified. For example, the Policy Studies Institute survey called *Black and*

White Britain (1984) stated that 29 per cent of Asians and 26 per cent of West Indians achieved 5 O Levels and more, compared with 24 per cent of the white population. However, the client still had an underlying personal belief that black people were unlikely to be qualified.

The ignorance which 'informs' what little research is done on black people as an audience is exasperating. I was asked to comment on some Aids research which seemed to suggest that while West Indians were wildly sexual, Asians were exactly the opposite. No one would accept London's East End as reliably representative of the UK as a whole, and yet underlying this research was an assumption that everyone belonging to each of these racial groups was exactly the same. There was no acknowledgment, for instance, that Asians have many different countries of origin, that some feel more integrated into British society than others, that some are more religious than others and that some are more ready than others to discard traditional ways of life.

The problem is that from an advertiser's point of view, images are competitive; corporate communications and brand maintenance campaigns are about reducing risks and unfortunately black people are often seen as a risk. We still live in an age where some retailers will not stock black hair products and cosmetics because they believe that more black customers means more shoplifting.

Let's suppose that BMW used an advert featuring a black male driving a BMW car; the questions that could be asked are: is the advert seen as just trying to reach black people? could it be seen as a black person's car? if you promote the car in this way, will the white consumer reject this 'black' image?

We cannot simply reject these hypothetical questions as racist. Advertisers are not in the charity business, nor is the sole purpose of their budget to give black people a better image. These questions need answers, and have often been the reason why black people who are featured in adverts are often blacks who already have a high profile and are well liked by the public, such as Daley Thompson or Frank Bruno. The risks of using these people are obviously lower. Agencies who promote specific black adverts to reach black people specifically are in danger of perpetuating these audience divisions.

Black people themselves do not want to be singled out as a special Advertising case, but they have questions and attitudes which need to be addressed. For example, we surveyed black people for their attitudes towards banks and financial institutions and the results showed a negative view: 'We have to overjustify ourselves', 'They do not trust us with money', 'They feel we have no track record in business'. A black face on a TV commercial for a bank may be a nice

73

thing, but does it answer any of these issues? Most black people would be more impressed by a white bank director saying something to the effect that they will be taken seriously by the bank, than by a token black appearance in an advert.

In America the perspective is different. 12.5 per cent of Americans are black, they have a longer history, a more developed and cohesive political base and therefore much more consumer power. It is the use of this power and of the threat of boycott which has advanced the black American position. Black people in the UK in the main have a short history, an embryonic political base and have yet to flex their muscles as consumers. They are also unimpressed by black American adverts.

The group research we have done has always indicated that black people feel they are portrayed in a negative light with no money, no job, no image, no self-esteem, no class. Most see advertising as a means to be seen in a more positive role, hence the frequent criticism of images on TV and radio, which always show black people always learning, never teaching; always subservient, never in authority.

If this is to change then advertisers and producers must be prepared to challenge these negative assumptions. Limited stereo-types can no longer be accepted as the whole truth, nor can adver-tisers continue to argue that their images simply reflect society when they are actually in the business of bucking trends. Deregulated broadcasting offers advertisers the chance to target audiences more effectively, but will their assumptions change?

THE DISABLED

A Teacher's Story

A diary written by Stephen Pegg for 'One Day in the Life of Television'

I am 40, six foot one in height, white, weigh just over 13 stone, have a wife, a daughter and an incurable illness. I have Motor Neurone Disease so cannot walk or write, am unable to dress or feed myself and rarely leave the house. Television is now an important part of my life, many of its images reminding me of recent normality.

This morning I watched two programmes for schools. *Seeing and Doing* (Channel Four) and *How We Used to Live* (Channel Four). I taught between 1967 and 1987 in Ruislip, Woolwich, Dagenham, Harefield, Eltham, Hartcliffe, Long Ashton and Nailsea. In all those places I sat with M1 or Class 6 or 'The Special Class', a lion tamer with a captive audience, and watched similar programmes.

Now that my speech is a dribbled slur, it's hard to recall how I controlled or cajoled every freckled Claire and Katie, pretty Jayne and Julie, naughty Wayne and Jason, knee-grazed Keith, mud-crazed David, quiet Ruth and round-eyed Ronnie, just Louis, Simon, Tim, Being anchored alone to record today's thoughts contrasts starkly with playground duty days shared with runners, stone-throwers, tale-tellers, skippers, swearers, sweet-sharers, hand-holders, coat-pullers, criers, shoelace-tiers, toy-takers, chasers, screamers, climbers and squealers, fighters and loners. Who'd have guessed I'd miss them so much?

During the afternoon I watched *Championship Bowls* and quiz programmes. When I was teaching I enjoyed organising sports and quizzes but now I am no longer coach or question-master. I am the spectator who always makes the best move or supplies the right answer. . . . I was watching bowls when my daughter Eleanor, four and three-quarters and escaped from school, burst through the door

75

clutching a crayon drawing of me in her left hand and a nearly-eaten Cornetto in her right hand.

I was enjoying a close game, so she went upstairs to watch children's television and my wife set the video to record Eleanor's Tuesday favourites, *The Sooty Show* and *Count Duckula* (ITV). At about 6 p.m., Eleanor returned to my room, took a large pillow from the bed and arranged it on my reclining chair, so that she could cuddle up between my knees and watch the recording of the same programmes she had seen an hour earlier. Before next Tuesday we will have viewed this tape at least four more times, Eleanor enjoying each incident as if it was brand new.

As I am now unable to take my daughter to a park, a swimming pool or theatre, and since I cannot play hide-and-seek or push her on a swing, read her stories or sing her songs, I treasure these moments spent together watching television. Ros fed me and Eleanor fell asleep near the end of *Count Duckula II*....

I viewed *The Mind Machine* (BBC 2) with mixed emotions, marvelling at the intricacy and energy of the brain yet being constantly reminded of my dwindling neurone reserves.... I had intended ending the day sitting up in bed watching bowls, but as my wife manoeuvred me from my wheelchair I slipped and fell to the floor. Ros was unable to lift me, so she telephoned for an ambulance and I lay there listening to the bowls and looking at the wall.

Soon after the game ended two ambulance men arrived. I was heaved on to the bed, 'goodnights' were exchanged, the television switched off, plugs were pulled, lights dimmed....

Blind Man's Buffer

John Donnelly

Television must by its very nature have only a limited appeal to the visually handicapped. I must stress at the very outset that although my observations are mainly subjective and confined to the effects of television on the totally blind individual, it is my experience that partially sighted people, even with a limited range of vision, can appreciate and enjoy television programmes.

The television set has become one of the most integral appliances in the modern household. Whatever the status or the earning capacity of the household the TV set is a must. Unfortunately, it has become such an institution in many houses, that once switched on, few people ever think of switching it off. Even the arrival of visitors is not allowed to interrupt the viewing and consequently conversation is punctuated by gaps when something on the 'box' arrests the attention of family or friends and few people regard this behaviour as bad-mannerly or smacking of ignorance. For the totally blind person, however, who has little interest or indeed knowledge of what is happening on the screen, the constant bombardment of disembodied voices, often facetious and interspersed with guffaws of forced laughter, can be annoying, sometimes even infuriating.

Perhaps blind people follow events in soaps just as avidly as their sighted counterparts, but I am convinced that many become involved in the activities of a certain 'Street' just for the sake of domestic tranquillity. The most suitable television programmes for the blind are probably documentaries or current affairs such as *World in Action* and *This Week*. There is usually sufficient dialogue in these programmes to enable the listener to follow events seen by the viewer and the same applies to news bulletins and some, but not all, quiz programmes. There are, however, many documentaries with too little dialogue and too many gaps, often interspersed with the sound of gunfire or of mob violence, to be of little use to the mere listener.

Golf, although it is very much a spectator sport, can be exciting because it is more amenable to description. Snooker is an unmitigated bore for anyone unable to see the action and cricket dies a death on television. Ball-by-ball commentaries of cricket and tennis and blow-by-blow coverage of boxing on radio are infinitely more suitable to the blind. Every move is fully described by experts who know the game inside out, and the flow of anecdotal information on the players, between the rallies, means that interest never flags. It seems, however, that radio and TV commentaries on soccer are poles apart. The radio commentator, however good, cannot fully describe or elaborate on the individual skills of the players for he must necessarily keep pace with the flow of the game, whereas the viewer can take everything in at a glance. Also the radio commentator is inclined to dramatise and create more excitement than some incidents really warrant. Horseracing is possibly the only sport where the two systems compete on more or less equal terms for they both provide an adequate commentary on the progress of the race.

Drama on television is particularly frustrating to the blind. Too little dialogue and changing scenes make it difficult for the listener to piece together action which is so obvious to the viewer and the sudden intrusion of advertisements into a programme, although clearly signalled to the viewer, often comes as a surprise to the listener. At a moment of high drama when the heroine is in deadly peril, the listener is suddenly startled to hear her being advised on how to get her undies whiter than white or her friends telling her they didn't know she had dandruff. The great difference between radio and TV drama is the narrator who sets the scene and paints the picture for the listener. For the viewer, the scene and the picture are already there making the narrator seem superfluous, even annoying.

Comedy also has its problems for the blind for most of the great comics rely largely on their appearance and facial expressions to create laughter. TV situation comedy leaves me cold and although the people watching it may be smiling, I seldom hear them laugh aloud, even with the aid of piped laughter. Music is, at least, the property of the listener and gains nothing from being presented on TV.

The fact of the matter would seem to be that TV relies on presenting its 'visible images' and as there is no substitute for sight, it will always remain an alien system of communication for the blind. If there is an answer it may lie in deregulation and in the possibility of greater selectivity and specialist programmes geared towards the blind as I believe is done for the deaf, that loneliest of all disabilities. This would have to incorporate some form of narration or some method of presenting an old-fashioned stage 'aside'. Until then, my personal solution to the problem is to slip into my own sanctuary, do my own thing, and let those who want to watch TV get on with it.

Is Anyone Listening?

Austin Reeves

In my opinion deaf people are the most neglected television viewers of all. Since I have been deaf from birth it's not surprising I hold this biased view, but the facts will bear me out.

By 'deaf' I mean anyone who cannot hear television dialogue properly. This includes those born profoundly deaf and those who become hard of hearing with encroaching age. A research project undertaken by the IBA in 1980 showed that 8 per cent of the total population were deaf – that's four million people in Britain. Most deaf people have low incomes and many are elderly. If we ignore cable and satellite, there are around 600 hours of TV programmes broadcast each week. Of that, only 10 per cent can be properly understood by deaf viewers with the help of Teletext subtitles, but since most deaf people don't have Teletext TV sets only one or two hours a week are accessible to them. In any event, there are large gaps in the types of programmes which have Teletext subtitles: only three news programmes have them; no current affairs or live shows are covered. On some evenings some of the channels have no subtitled programmes at all.

What are the difficulties deaf people face? For reasons I don't understand, some people seem to think lipreading is easy. It isn't. Lipreading is largely a matter of intelligent guesswork as we try to fit words we don't understand around those we do. Have a go at lipreading 'mat', 'pat' and 'bat'. I am considered a good lipreader, but there's no way I can see the difference between those three words. Once a word is put into its context, it's easier to work out whether or not it's correct, but that leads to another problem. We spend so much effort trying to work out what the words are that there is little or no time to understand their meanings. Even in the best conditions – with good light, or in one-to-one conversation, for example – it's still difficult. Television compounds every difficulty.

The major problem for us is how people on television speak. After all, they are talking to 'the general public', not to an individual who is deaf. Think about the way you talk to deaf people and you will realise that your speech does change: you make it louder and slower, or you repeat words. You make an effort to make yourself understood. Speakers on television, through no fault of their own, do not do that. They speak too fast, or they mumble, they don't always face the camera and quite often speak off-screen. This is bad enough for those of us who cannot hear at all, but even for those with some minor loss of hearing, background sounds often drown the speaker's voice.

Can you remember during the Falklands War when a certain civil servant always held the Press Conference? He gave information in a slow and deliberate manner. For the first time in my life I could understand everything. He was absolutely brilliant and would probably have still been all right if he'd spoken a bit faster. Of course the 'general public' thought he was too slow. We just can't win!

These are some of the reasons why deaf people cannot fully benefit from TV. The solution is to make the dialogue visible through subtitles or sign language. The sounds on some programmes could also be made clearer. The majority of broadcasters do not appreciate the importance of these obvious points – perhaps it suits them to ignore them.

Why should we be concerned? It's true, after all that there are other sources of entertainment and information, but the evidence tells us that television and radio are easily the most popular ones amongst the general public. Four million deaf people very much want to belong to that public. We pay the same licence fee and are 'persuaded' by some adverts to part with our money, but we don't have the same choice as everyone else. Magazine programmes made especially for the deaf are very valuable but we want to be able to enjoy standard programmes like *Emmerdale Farm* or *Tomorrow's World* along with our hearing friends and relatives, we want to be able to talk about them with our workmates the next day. We find this lack of choice frustrating and it can be embarrassing when deaf people are expected to be grateful for small mercies.

I know that it's also frustrating for subtitlers who know that they should be doing far more but are restricted by lack of resources. Sign language is a different issue – many broadcasters refuse to accept it because they consider it too distracting. We've never argued, however, that there should be sign language in every programme. We don't want to see interpreters on *EastEnders*, but sign language should be used on news and information programmes, and of course on those programmes made especially for deaf viewers.

In fact, some IBA research in the Tyne Tees area showed that ordinary viewers were prepared to accept sign language on some programmes, but broadcasters refused to acknowledge the validity of these findings, continuing to argue that sign language was too distracting and that in any event the findings of a local survey could not be applied nationally. It seems to me that broadcasters are more concerned about the prettiness of their pictures than they are about making a range of good quality programmes which everyone can enjoy. But then there are no regulations which say that broadcasters must make their programmes accessible to all viewers.

What have we tried to do about this? The Deaf Broadcasting Council (DBC), formed in 1980, has been trying to make TV more accessible to deaf people. We've had a hard battle for ten years, often feeling that we are bashing against brick walls. I think it would be true to say that people find it difficult to understand our aims because they can't actually imagine what it is like to be deaf. Our work has to be persuasive. We succeeded in getting a clause in the Cable and Broadcasting Act of 1984 which stated that Cable TV operators should consider the needs of deaf people. To date, not one operator has done anything positive because the clause was voluntary, not mandatory. That experience taught us to make our demands much stronger, which is why 1989/90, with the government's Broadcasting Bill, is an extremely important period for us. The DBC is concerned that the increasing number of commercial TV channels will mean even less attention and fewer resources given to services for minority audiences, so we must take the opportunities to lobby for positive requirements to be inserted into the Bill.

The only mention of deaf people's needs in the White Paper referred to the value of Teletext subtitles. The DBC submitted two main resolutions and 31 recommendations. We called for a mandatory clause to provide services for the deaf or hard of hearing, providing them with equality of opportunity for access to all channels, whether cable, satellite or terrestrial. By access we mean mainly Teletext subtitles but also include in-vision subtitles (like those for *Newsview*), and sign language on selected programmes. We also called for timetabled implementation of the clause to ensure that six months after the Act, 25 per cent of all programmes would be made accessible and that 100 per cent accessibility should be achieved within five years. We are aiming for the ultimate. It's not unreasonable to ensure that anyone can switch on the TV and be confident that they will be able to understand it.

Since the government had already decided that Channel 3 must produce high quality news and have a regional remit, why should it not include access for deaf viewers? We resolved that Channels 3 and 5 should be obliged to broadcast a diverse service including educational and minority programmes, spread across the schedules so that no specialised services are totally marginalised. The importance of specialised programmes on BBC, on Channel Four and in the smaller ITV regions should also be safeguarded.

We recommended that the ITC and the Broadcasting Standards Council be given responsibility for safeguarding the requirements of deaf viewers, and called for equality of opportunity in employment and participation in broadcasting to be extended to disabled people.

At first the government refused to accept their responsibility, arguing that, constitutionally, it lies with the broadcasters. We countered this by emphasising that we were referring not to programme content but to the *structure* of broadcasting. It was heartening when in June the Home Secretary agreed that Parliament should decide on the proportion of Teletext subtitles Channels 3 and 5 will have to produce. This marks an important step forward because a principle has now been established – Parliament *is* responsible. However, the government proposes a 10 per cent increase in Teletext services – an extra 1.5 hours a week. This is peanuts, and there are other important areas still being ignored. We must continue with our lobbying.

If we are successful, deaf viewers will at last become, through television, more equal members of society. We could be part of the television's 'general public' and no longer a minority. A great dream, isn't it?

Invisible People: The Disabled on Television

Timothy Leggatt

This chapter will draw upon research recently carried out by the Broadcasting Research Unit into the portrayal on television of people with disabilities. As part of the research, people with disabilities, as well as members of the general public, were asked about the portrayal of disabled people on television. Discussion groups were also held with disabled people in order to obtain a clearer idea of their opinions.[1] In discussing what disabled people think about the provision made for them as a special section of the television audience, particular attention will be paid here to what they think of their appearances on television, of how often they appear, and in what guise. This is because in every circumstance disabled people quite emphatically wish to be treated like other people in our society. While they want broadcasters to make some special provision for their own minority interests, in so far as these may occasionally differ from those of the audience as a whole, they also want the society depicted on television to include minorities, representing all its members.

The first point to make is that disabled people are indeed a neglected audience. Our research showed that the public at large is fully aware that a substantial minority of people suffer from disabilities of one kind or another, and since the Census Office tells us that disabled people constitute 14 per cent of the British population, they might expect to see people like themselves regularly appearing on television. The disabled people in our survey (that is, those registered as disabled, or who consider themselves to have a permanent disability) were asked how often they saw people with disabilities in different genres of television programmes. Of those who answered, 81 per cent said they never, or hardly ever, saw disabled people appearing in quiz shows; 80 per cent said the same of soap operas and 73 per cent said the same of situation comedies. In contrast, only 37 per cent said they never, or hardly ever saw disabled people appear in sports programmes and only 15 per cent said the same about documentaries.

Of the disabled respondents to our survey, 63 per cent agreed with the opinion that there are too few drama programmes on television which feature people with disabilities; 70 per cent also agreed that people with disabilities should appear on all types of programmes; 81 per cent disagreed with the opinion that disabled people should only appear on TV programmes produced especially for them.

In the world as represented on television, people with disabilities are almost invisible. Although they are occasionally featured in news, current affairs and magazine programmes, disabled people seldom appear in soaps, quiz shows and sitcoms. Television certainly fails to give people with disabilities their due in terms of their presence in the population at large. Disabled people also often find their portrayal on television unacceptable, sentimental and patronising. They dislike the ways in which disabled characters are so often introduced into feature films: as criminals, as inadequate people or added simply to enhance a menacing atmosphere or a scene of deprivation.

Our findings also revealed that more disabled than able-bodied people admit to feeling embarrassed when watching severely disabled people on television. Of the disabled people questioned, 24 per cent said they felt embarrassed on certain occasions, whereas of the entire group only 18 per cent expressed this view. Similarly, 47 per cent of the disabled group agreed that some disabilities are 'too disturbing and should *not* be shown on television', in contrast to 38 per cent of the whole group surveyed.

It is evidently quite misleading to treat everyone with a disability as an homogeneous group. 'The disabled' can be defined according to the nature (and sometimes to the severity) of the disabilities they suffer, and then again, according to whether their disablement is defined in medical or social terms. There are, for example, great differences between the experiences of the wheelchair-bound and the hard of hearing, or the diabetic. The person in a wheelchair has become the emblem of disability, making a range of disadvantages quite visible and thus providing a convenient shorthand for television. Mobility problems, mental defects and other conspicuous handicaps such as blindness, figure more extensively in television's representation of disabled people than they should do, because they are more easily portrayed. For others, whose disabilities are less visible – diabetics or epileptics, for example – this emphasis is unsubtle and uncaring, if not insulting.

Those who generally accept a medical definition of their disablement (which is how disability is defined by the Census Office) may not consider that provision for the disabled on television, nor its representations of the disabled are deficient. In sharp contrast, the group that considers disability to be socially defined will regard broadcasters as bearing some responsibility for television's impoverished representations and provision. This group sees the attitudes and reactions of able-bodied people to their experience as a significant factor in causing their disablement. For example, if access to social facilities is inadequate for some disabled people, then they consider themselves 'disabled' *because of this inadequate provision*, which is almost invariably made by able-bodied people. The defining role of able-bodied people is quite clear in cases such as the provision of access, but it can extend beyond material conditions into attitudes and ideas. The group which considers their disabilities to be socially defined will tend to say that society (by which they mean the able-bodied) treats them not as people who happen to have disabilities, but as *disabled people*. In other words society sees the disability rather than the person, and acts accordingly. From this viewpoint disabled people are consequently treated in peculiar ways, not least by television.

When the portrayal of disabled people on factual programmes is (as is often the case) sentimental in character, inviting the response 'Isn't she/he brave? Isn't she/he wonderful in overcoming her/his disability?', there will therefore be different reactions. Some disabled people will accept that this kind of portrayal is at least friendly, if not compassionate, whereas others will see it as condescending if not downright insulting.

What is to be done, given that on television people with disabilities are under-represented and are treated more often as a special category than as ordinary people? If we recognise the substantial dependence many disabled people have on television then this question has to be confronted. Responsibility lies with writers, editors and producers and also with us, able-bodied and disabled members of the audience, for allowing this deplorable state of affairs to continue.

Of course writers' creativity must be allowed to flourish and editorial independence preserved, but professional broadcasters need to be more concerned that their total output reasonably reflects and reacts to the whole society in which they live and work. They must respond more positively to the demands disabled people are making of television. There should be enough of us in the audience who are not prepared to put up with how television depicts the world, who will press for change in broadcasting to ensure that the disabled audience is no longer neglected but depicted in a spirit which is both compassionate and generous.

Note
1 Guy Cumberbatch and Ralph Negrine: *The Portrayal of People with Disabilities on Television*, Broadcasting Research Unit (forthcoming).

Seeing Through TV: Children Talking About Television

David Buckingham

While it might well be argued that broadcasters have neglected children as an audience, it could scarcely be said that media researchers have done the same. On the contrary, there has been an enormous amount of research into the relationship between children and television, albeit largely confined to a rather limited range of issues. Yet in a sense, there has been a kind of neglect here too – a neglect of children's own perspectives, and a failure to consider their responses to the medium in their own terms.

Traditionally, both research and public debate about children and television have been preoccupied with identifying the allegedly harmful effects of viewing. The perennial issue of 'violence' – itself a notoriously imprecise term – has been the most sensational aspect of this concern, but television has been accused of causing a whole catalogue of social and psychological ills. Apart from being suspected of producing delinquent and anti-social behaviour, television is also regarded as a negative influence on children's emotional and intellectual development, and a major source of undesirable ideologies and beliefs.

Children are seen as particularly vulnerable to these negative effects, largely because they lack the cognitive 'defences' which are possessed by adults. Thus, it is argued, children are unable to tell the difference between fiction and reality, or between commercials and programmes. They often fail to perceive what researchers or producers regard as the main points of an argument, or the connections between different stages of a narrative. They are ignorant of the ways in which programmes are produced, and of many of the conventions

87

of the medium, and as a result they often make confused or inaccurate interpretations of what they watch. Children are thus defined as viewers in terms of what they lack: they are uncritical, unselective, indiscriminate and irrational.

There are a number of problems with this view. The methods researchers have traditionally used to gather evidence – such as laboratory experiments and questionnaires – have led them to ignore or suppress children's own interpretations and judgments of their viewing, and the processes by which these are produced. In theoretical terms, the dominant view remains a behaviourist one: children are effectively regarded as 'blank slates' on which television scrawls its harmful messages.

All too often, researchers have implicitly treated 'children' as a homogeneous category, without differentiating between different age groups, or accounting for the role of social factors such as class, gender or ethnic background. Children's interpretations of television have been judged (and found wanting) in comparison with an 'adult' norm, rather than investigated in their own terms. Ultimately, the dominant view of children as an audience severely underestimates their existing understandings and abilities, and drastically oversimplifies the complexity of the viewing process.

In common with some recent research,[1] the work reported here seeks to construct a different agenda. It is not concerned with measuring the 'effects' of television viewing, nor with making judgments about whether it is harmful or beneficial. On the contrary, it is concerned with much more fundamental questions about how children 'read' or construct meaning from television, and how they negotiate these meanings with others. The research starts from the view that this is a social process, which is both complex and highly variable. Its primary focus is on small-group talk, rather than observations of children in laboratories or responses to questionnaires: it does not aim to code and quantify a product, but to describe and analyse a process. Certainly at this stage, it is research which seeks to generate questions and to inform more theoretical speculation, rather than to offer definitive proof.

The research I shall describe was undertaken in the spring and summer of 1989, as a pilot study for a much more extensive and systematic project.[2] It was based on a series of discussions which took place in a small primary school in Hackney, East London, with groups of children aged between eight and eleven. A total of 47 children took part, some on a number of occasions, and in a variety of combinations. The topics for discussion and the programmes we viewed were determined largely by the children themselves.

It was certainly my aim to make the discussions as open-ended as possible, and to avoid imposing my own agenda. Nevertheless, it would be false to suppose that this kind of research is straightfor-wardly 'naturalistic'. What children say in any situation does not necessarily correspond in any simple way to what they 'really' think, and should never be taken at face value. Any adult asking questions about television, particularly in a school context, is inevitably going to invite certain 'approved', adult ways of speaking – and in particu-lar what I would term a distanced or 'critical' discourse about television.

There was certainly plenty of evidence of this in the children's discussions. In terms of national viewing figures, 8–11 year olds watch more television than almost any other age group, yet there was little evidence that these children watched indiscriminately or unse-lectively. While there were clear favourites shared by most children – particularly serials such as *Neighbours*, *EastEnders* and *Grange Hill* – the range of programmes they enjoyed was diverse and extensive. Very few of the children claimed that their parents regulated their viewing in any way, beyond imposing bedtimes: most were familiar with a whole range of 'adult' programmes, and many had seen '18'-rated videotapes. Across the discussions, more than a hundred pro-grammes or films were mentioned, ranging from *Blue Peter* to *Nightmare on Elm Street*, from *Blind Date* to *The News*. Certain genres emerged as favourites – particularly soaps, sitcoms, cartoons and comedy/horror films – although within these, there were some fine distinctions made: *Neighbours* was preferred to its rival *Home and Away*, *EastEnders* to its rivals *Coronation Street* and *Brookside*, *Ghostbusters* to *Masters of the Universe*, *The Cosby Show* to *Bread*.

Neither was there evidence that television programmes are merely enjoyed and then quickly forgotten. In one discussion, a group of ten-year-olds was able to recall no fewer than ten episodes of *The Cosby Show*; and there were numerous instances of detailed, line-by-line retellings of favourite programmes and films, often accompanied by mime and sound effects. In the case of *Grange Hill*, children recalled events that had taken place many years previously, in almost nostalgic tones.

While the children remain strongly loyal to programmes they enjoy, their preferences are constantly evolving, and there was con-siderable debate about the relative merits of particular programmes. Even clear favourites like *Neighbours* could be subject to some quite harsh critical commentary, and often to ridicule. Poor acting, failed attempts at humour, weak storylines and cheap production values would be tolerated, but only up to a point. Yet while the children did discriminate between programmes, often in quite rigorous and exacting ways, their idea of 'quality' was rather more diverse than that of many adults: children certainly demand quality, but they also demand variety and choice.

The children's allegiances to particular programmes are also bound up with their sense of self, and their relationships with others. In many cases, they made clear judgments about which programmes were 'for them', and which were 'too babyish' or obviously 'for grown-ups'. In the case of programmes which were seen as clearly gender-specific – for example, the action-adventure cartoons favoured by some younger boys and condemned by most of the girls – there was often considerable pressure within the group to maintain the boundary between 'boys' programmes' and 'girls' programmes'. Nevertheless, many genres which critics have identified as gender-specific did not appear to be perceived in this way: many of the girls described gory horror films with great relish, while most of the boys were quite ready to discuss the romantic entanglements of soap opera characters.

In the case of genres with which they were very familiar, the children displayed a lucid understanding of codes and conventions. In discussing soap operas, for example, the children were clearly aware of the role of the cliffhanger and of multiple narratives in sustaining their involvement:

> *Cissy* (8): [On *Neighbours*] It's got a good way of acting it out. They always keep you in suspense when it ends, so you have to see the next part, and you can't miss it, so you're always wanting to see the next part. . . . They've made it exciting, like they've made all the characters do different things and then they have other characters in for a few days or something . . . so it doesn't get boring with only a few people.

Similarly, in predicting future developments, the children would often speculate about the possibility of characters being written out – although in the case of *Neighbours* this was also informed by their knowledge of current developments in the serial in Australia, which is a year-and-a-half ahead of the UK.

On the other hand, in the case of action-adventure cartoons, the narrative structure was seen by most of the children as entirely predictable, and indeed as being motivated by a rather simplistic morality:

> *Gaynor* (10): The person who's done the cartoon has made it so the goodies always win, so the baddies don't. But the baddies just, like, get a bit of their own way . . .

DB: So why do you think they do that?
Gaynor: To prove . . . to prove that you shouldn't always be bad or you're going to get something turned back to you. So you should be good.

Colin (11) likened the narratives of these cartoons to those of fairy tales, in which the characters always live 'happy ever after': while they lacked an explicit moral, they had a similarly predictable ending, and were thus seen to be quite clearly aimed at younger children.

Similarly, the children often displayed an ironical awareness of television as an artefact – as something which has been deliberately produced, rather than merely a 'slice of life'. In the case of fictional programmes, they consistently referred to the quality of the acting, and there were numerous references to cameras, scripts and studio sets.

Cissy (8): In *Neighbours*, when they walk out of the door of houses, like, they've only got a picture behind. It's not real houses, you know.

The children were not slow to note continuity mistakes and inconsistencies in characters' behaviour. The change in the actor playing Lucy in *Neighbours*, for example, attracted considerable ridicule, if not quite as much hilarity as the birth of Daphne's baby:

Chvonne (10): And when Daphne had her baby, she kept her tights on!

These latter judgments relate to a broader preoccupation with the modality of television – that is, the extent to which it is perceived as 'realistic' – which recurred throughout these discussions. In the case of genres which are by definition 'unrealistic' – such as cartoons, and to a certain extent comedy and horror – this is less of an issue, although these can on occasion be ridiculed for this reason. The ability of cartoon superheroes to recover instantly from seemingly fatal attacks, or the inevitability with which they snatch victory from the jaws of defeat, were seen by many as merely tedious and routine. For some of the older children, maintaining a constant running commentary on the implausibility and indeed the sheer physical impossibility of the action seemed to offer a means of distancing themselves from programmes which were generally seen as much too 'babyish'.

In the case of horror films, which were a particular favourite of many children, there was much discussion of the quality of the special effects. Detailed re-enactments of brains being splattered against walls, skin melting in acid, and arms and testicles being blown off were accompanied by an extensive repertoire of sound effects. Any sense of the narrative context was lost in favour of a wildly enthusiastic (and almost incomprehensible) rehearsal of the 'good bits'. Yet apart from recalling the pleasure of being shocked and frightened, the children were also interested in speculating about how particular effects were achieved, and some reported rewinding tapes 'to see if you can see any trickery'.

However, with programmes which offer representations much closer to the children's lived experience, their discussion of modality is often more complex and sophisticated. In the case of *Grange Hill*, for example, they recognised that the need for realism and plausibility has to be balanced against the need to entertain and engage the viewer with dramatic or comic storylines. The children felt that secondary school would be like *Grange Hill* to a certain extent, although they acknowledged that many of the less dramatic aspects (notably 'work') had been omitted, and that much of the action was implausible. There was also considerable speculation about the relationship between the actors and the characters they played: were they 'meant to be like that' or were they not also 'a bit like that in real life'?

Likewise, the family in *The Cosby Show* was seen as both 'ordinary' and 'extraordinary'. While the children regarded the Huxtable family's problems as similar to their own, they were also aware that the family was much more wealthy than theirs, and felt that the parents were somewhat idealised:

Kerry (10): But no parents look after their children in that way. The children wouldn't talk about their problems so much to the grown-ups because . . . know what I mean, in that programme they find it so easy just to go and tell their mum and dad, but it's not always that easy. So in some ways it's not realistic.

Despite this, at least some of the children did seem willing to use the programme as a source of 'good advice': 'If I found myself in a situation like that, I'd remember about all the things I've seen about that, and how much trouble you can get into' (Kate, 10). While the comedy elements in *The Cosby Show* were seen to detract from this – and particularly the knowledge that problems would always be resolved by the end of the programme – they did not wholly undermine it, as they were seen to do in *Bread*:

Kerry (10): It's just made to make you laugh, it's not made to make you think about what's happening in families. You're just meant to watch it and listen to the jokes.

In certain instances, this concern with modality extended to a discussion of representation – that is, of the extent to which the people or situations portrayed can be seen as representative of the social world more broadly. *The Cosby Show* provoked considerable discussion of the representation of black people on television, which was generally seen as inadequate and patronising, by black and white children alike. Programmes like *Dallas* and *Dynasty* were condemned for their lack of black characters, while *EastEnders* was seen as reserving its most dramatic storylines for the white characters.

Kate (10): I don't think they actually *look* for black people to be in their programmes. I don't think they even try and get them. I don't think they want them either.

Even 'black' programmes like *Desmond's* were seen as lacking in authenticity:

Derek (11): I know real Jamaicans, they don't even speak like that. They speak wrong. The feelings, when they say it, it's different.

At the same time, many of the children resented the segregation of black people into almost exclusively 'black' programmes like *The Cosby Show*:

Kerry (10): That's bad, if you have a programme for black people and [one for] white people. Because the black people would feel a bit ashamed if they got white friends. They should just mix it.

What is also quite notable here is the children's awareness of agency – in other words, of the fact that television programmes are produced by groups of people with particular motivations, with a view to reaching particular audiences and encouraging them to respond in particular ways. This was most evidently the case in the children's discussions of advertising, where the motivations of advertisers were regarded with considerable scepticism. The children were clearly aware that advertisements are intended not merely to inform, but to persuade people to buy, and they were repeatedly accused of dishonesty in the process. The children volunteered numerous stories about products they had purchased which had not lived up to the claims made about them in adverts, and speculated about how the advertisers faked the tests and surveys which were used to promote the claims of washing powders or cat foods.

At the same time, the children's responses to particular adverts were in many cases wildly enthusiastic, even in the case of products they themselves would never have purchased, such as pensions or petrol. Their appreciation of advertisements and of products themselves seemed to be quite independent of each other, to the extent that they were often unable to remember the name of the products, while they could recall the advertisement in considerable detail:

> *Garry* (8): Some people think that adverts are to make them ... buy it. But the advert is just, like, for watching. Some people love the advert but they never buy it.

Likewise, the discussion of cartoons was marked by a similar degree of cynicism about the producers' motivations, and in particular about their exaggerated gender stereotyping. The occasional presence of female superheroes was seen merely as tokenism:

> *Colin* (11): They made *He-Man* first, but I reckon that people were saying that it was sexist and everything. So they made *She-Ra*.

As the girls were quick to point out, *She-Ra* could not be seen as equal or equivalent to *He-Man*: while they clearly felt that having 'strong' female characters was a positive development, they argued that She-Ra was still seen in relation to He-Man, rather than as an independent character, and that she rarely encountered 'real baddies'.

Despite their often vociferous criticisms of television, it was notable that the children did not perceive themselves to be at risk from any potential harm it might cause. While they were certainly aware of popular discourses about the 'effects' of television, these effects were significantly displaced on to those much younger than themselves:

> *Colin* (11): It's because ... little children. Like my mate, his little brother, he's two and he watches it [*Thundercats*]. And that's why they don't put nobody getting killed or nothing at the end ... Because they'll be going about, and if somebody hit them or something, they'll be going 'I'm gonna kill you!' and everything. It will put hate in their hearts.

While they would occasionally admit to imitating what they watched themselves, the children were quick to point out that this had taken place many years previously, and certainly when they were no older than two. Just as for adults, it is always 'other people' who are seen to be at risk.

In putting together this brief account of the research, I have inevitably been highly selective. Research of this kind quickly produces enormous amounts of data, which does not easily lend itself to generalisations. My selection has not been arbitrary, however: I have deliberately emphasised the 'critical' aspects of these children's discussions, and their often complex understanding of the medium. This emphasis has been designed to serve a polemical purpose. Given the dominance of the 'effects' approach, with its definition of children as passive and lacking in 'viewing skills', I have sought to offer a contrary view of children as active, critical, sophisticated viewers.

In the current context of debate about children and television, I would see this as a necessary emphasis. Nevertheless, it is only a starting point. It is not enough simply to describe or report what children say, as I have done here. We need to analyse why and how these kinds of 'critical' judgments are produced, and the functions they serve.

Thus, the extent to which children engage in this kind of 'critical' reading will depend upon a number of interrelated factors. Children's access to different ways of talking about television will obviously depend on social and developmental factors. They will engage with different programmes or genres in different ways, for example according to whether they are seen as more or less 'realistic'. What children say in this kind of situation will depend upon their relationship with others in the group and on their perception of the motivations of the researcher.

For all these reasons, we cannot simply accept what children say at face value, as a straightforward reflection of what they think. Children may well 'know' things they find it unnecessary to say, or which they are unable or unwilling to articulate in certain situations. They may attempt to please or impress the interviewer or other individuals in the group, but they may equally do the opposite, again for a variety of reasons. Future research will need to be much more sensitive to the complex and often contradictory ways in which meanings are established and negotiated in talk.

Beyond this, there is clearly a danger in this kind of research of implicitly validating certain kinds of reading at the expense of others. My selective account of the discussions has deliberately sought to demonstrate that children are just as capable of making 'critical' judgments about television as adults. In this respect, I have continued to compare children's responses with an 'adult' norm. Yet it is questionable whether adults are in fact consistently 'critical' viewers, and indeed whether it is possible or even desirable that they should be.

In making my selection, I have excluded a large amount of data which displays quite different qualities. In discussing their favourite programmes and characters, in recounting the plots and acting out the 'good bits', these children speak in a much less inhibited way about their *emotional* engagement with television, and about the pleasures they experience from it. This is not necessarily incompatible with the more rational kind of judgment I have identified, but it is, for many adults, precisely where the problem lies: for it is through its immediate emotional pleasures that television is believed to exert its evil effects.

To focus on children's capacities as 'critical', sophisticated viewers may well be reassuring to those who are anxious about the dangerous pleasures of television. Yet it may also lead us to neglect a good deal of what is important about it – for adults as well as for children. In terms of research, it would seem to be vital to take account of everything children say, not simply where they seem to be telling us what they think we want to hear.

Notes

1. For example, Bob Hodge and David Tripp, *Children and Television* (Cambridge: Polity Press, 1986); Patricia Palmer, *The Lively Audience* (Sydney: Allen and Unwin, 1986); David Buckingham, *Public Secrets: 'EastEnders' and its Audience* (London: British Film Institute, 1987).
2. I am grateful to the Institute of Education, University of London, for a small research grant which made this work possible, and to Peter Sanders, Jackie Simmonds and Richard Lewis for allowing me access to their classrooms. The research continues in the form of a project on 'The Development of Television Literacy', funded by the Economic and Social Research Council, which began in October 1989.

Children's Television After 1992

David Elstein

Until 1988, every major change in the television environment had been preceded by substantial public debate about the rationale behind the change and its potential impact. The 1990 Broadcasting Act will transform British television, but the public debate that has taken place so far has been limited to narrow issues: the funding of Channel Four, the auctioning of ITV, whilst missing the wider picture.

In 1993, Channel Five will start transmissions. It will have almost immediate access, at little or no charge to the consumer, to 70 per cent of the population. Whereas with BBC 1, ITV, BBC 2 and Channel Four there was a clear expectation that the arrival of a new channel would broaden the range of television, Channel Five has been consigned to pure commercialism by governmental decree. It will have almost no obligations, other than to make a profit.

The potential impact on other channels is huge. With Channel Four simultaneously being cut adrift financially from ITV, and with the ITV system itself subject to substantial change as the pressure to fulfil auction pledges brings itself to bear within a much looser regulatory frame, the 'protected areas' of the commercial television system are bound to be put at substantial risk.

It is therefore hard to suppress one's incredulity that the Broadcasting Minister (then Timothy Renton) should confidently inform Parliament in the summer of 1989 that 'we see no reason why high quality children's programmes, sustained by viewer demand, should not continue to flourish on British television after 1992.' Mr Renton's disingenuous argument, in resisting calls for children's programming to be protected by specific provisions in the new Act, was that they were not currently protected yet still flourished under the

97

IBA regime. Furthermore there is no evidence to suppose that the new Minister, David Mellor, sees any need for further intervention.

This ignores the fact that the IBA currently has the power to disapprove the ITV schedule in each and every aspect, and uses that power to require not just a minimum amount of children's programming, but within it a real variety of drama, information and entertainment; such that animation, either home-produced or imported, constitutes only a minority element of the schedule. ITV also continues to produce and transmit pre-school programmes of high quality even though, in strictly commercial terms, parents of under-fives constitute only a small proportion of the audience available to view them when they are broadcast.

A more lightly regulated system, operating under an Act which does not give children's programmes specific protection, is highly unlikely to be able to deliver what the current system can. The proposed ITC, which will auction the ITV franchises, may insist that applicants commit themselves to given hours of children's output, and even given levels of expenditure, but the power to intervene on detailed scheduling issues will have been removed. New contractors will, therefore, quickly come to terms with the commercial realities of the post-1992 market.

Even now, children's programmes generate much less revenue in proportion to their cost than the rest of the ITV schedule (in my rough estimate, five times less!). From 4.00 to 5.15 p.m., when children's programmes are shown on ITV and BBC 1 every weekday, is the one time-slot in the week when the joint audience share of those two channels consistently drops below 70 per cent. Once Channel Five (and the new satellite operators, if they achieve sufficient penetration) adds its competitive weight to Channel Four and BBC 2 in targeting adult programming in that time slot (such as Australian or American day-time soaps), the two-channel audience share will drop much further, perhaps to 50 per cent or less.

The pressure then will be to squeeze every last drop of revenue out of the child audience that is not either watching adult fare or is prevented from watching children's programmes by adults watching adult fare. Even if the current level of spending on children's weekday programming on ITV (£30 millions a year) were mandatory to the new contractors and imposed by the ITC during the auction, the commercial pressure would be to spend nearly all that money on high-cost, high-rating UK-produced animation, to intersperse with bought-in animation. The knock-on impact on the BBC would be considerable. It would not be long before our children's schedule resembled the 'animation and fun' deserts of the US networks. The brutal commercial truth is that children are not a sufficiently rich advertising market to justify spending more than a limited amount of money on a limited range of programmes for narrowly defined time-slots, unless a regulator forces commercial operators to do otherwise.

It is no comfort to talk of 'viewer demand' sustaining 'high quality children's programmes'. If advertiser-supported services cannot do this, the Minister can only be referring to subscriber services. Indeed in America, operations such as Disney and Nickelodeon do provide a service somewhat better than the networks' but they are, of course, only available to the children in that small fraction of US households which choose to or can afford to, subscribe.

It would be a massive step backwards for this country socially and culturally if quality children's programming were removed from free-TV and only available on the BBC and pay-TV. For, in such circumstances, as BBC executives readily admit, the BBC service would suffer a double squeeze: in ratings from an animation-driven ITV, and in quality as the competitive edge generated by the present ITV service disappeared.

The looming crisis ironically comes at a time when ITV is making a determined effort to re-shape and revitalise its children's output. The recent 30 per cent increase in its share of 10–15 year-old child viewers reflects the concentration on particular types of drama and entertainment. *Home and Away* has been added to the schedule to pick up the older children and teenagers who have made a cult of *Neighbours*. Even so, there are still advertisers who feel ITV must and can do better, in their terms! But unless the children's audience is to be favoured at the expense of the far richer adult audience – a deeply improbable scenario in a post-1992 lightly-regulated commercial sector – the only outcome that is likely to emerge is the one I have already described: money and effort concentrated into an increasingly narrowing range.

Against the commercial imperatives, only legislation, or ITC powers to intervene far beyond those currently envisaged, will be effective: but where is the public debate, or the parliamentary lobby, which will protect the quality of what our children watch?

Missing Opportunities

Jim Marshall

During the last ten years the television medium and particularly commercial television has undergone something of a quiet revolution. Since November 1982, when Channel Four was launched, ITV has developed into a 24-hour service, adding breakfast time television (TV-am), morning time television and transmissions throughout the night. Channel Four is also moving in that direction and is now off air only during the small hours of the morning. Consequently, since the beginning of the 80s transmission hours on commercial television have almost tripled.

The television set, traditionally to be found in the front room, used to be the focal point for the entire family's entertainment. Now many homes, certainly those containing families, have or are in the process of upgrading their equipment to include VCRs, teletext and videogames usually operated with a remote control. And, most importantly, those homes usually have more than one television set, ensuring that the various members of the family can all watch what particularly interests them.

Not surprisingly the programming policy of the television companies reflects this opportunity for greater freedom in viewing across the different sectors of the population. While ITV continues to transmit, during the main body of the evening at least, programmes likely to appeal to a wide sector of the population, Channel Four endeavours to cater for a differing range of audiences and their specific interests. In this recent scramble to offer much more to everybody, how have children fared?

Unlike the city broker or the nineteen-year-old, the child is the perfect consumer of the television medium and indeed the advertising message carried on commercial television. They are avid viewers

of good programming, though totally dismissive of poor programmes. From a remarkably early age children can assimilate an
advertising message considerably more quickly than adults. Their
sociable nature also ensures that the message is relayed to friends and
parents.

Television seems to have everything going for it in terms of
programming and advertising opportunities for children. But there
are some serious flaws. Ironically, children are poorly served by
commercial television and the advertising opportunities, or at least
cost-effective ones, are limited. Irrespective of quality, the main
problem with child programming is that there is just too little of it.

ITV and Channel Four now transmit over 250 hours of programming a week. Of that total, child programming amounts to less than
ten per cent, some 25 hours of programmes specifically designed for
children, per week. It is hard to see how this amount can effectively
cater for the different age groups, let alone cover the varying interests
of the children within each age group.

Assessing the quality of child programmes is a hazardous exercise
because the child audience is fickle, diverse in its interests and highly
unpredictable. There is the added problem of designing programmes
for the different age groups: the definition of children as being
anyone between the ages of four and fifteen is far too broad. But even
allowing for these difficulties, commercial television's track record
for child programmes is poor.

The BBC has for some years transmitted the highest rating programmes for all children. Admittedly ITV has a fairly good track
record with their programmes for younger children, but programmes designed specifically for older age groups do not perform
well. In contrast the BBC have consistently shown that programming
for the older age groups is not a hopeless task with *Grange Hill*, the
perennial *Blue Peter* and various drama series such as the *Chronicles
of Narnia*, all achieving high audiences.

Interestingly, ITV's top ten programmes for children includes a
number of adult programmes, such as *Coronation Street* which
generally appears in the top five. This is not a reflection of the
strength of adult programmes on ITV, but rather an indication of the
paltry number of child programmes. (See Tables 1 and 2.)

The poor performance of ITV and Channel Four's programmes
shows that insufficient resources are allocated to children's programming. Does it really matter? The cynical view is that commercial TV
is unlikely to win the ratings battle by showing children's programmes and, from an advertising revenue perspective, the child is
deemed to be the least important consumer.

But the cynical view is ill-informed. Total child viewing peaks at

TABLE 1
Top Children TVR Programmes – Including Repetitions
October 1989

Programme	Channel	Day	TVRS
1. Neighbours	BBC1	Monday	38
2. Neighbours	BBC1	Friday	36
3. Neighbours	BBC1	Thursday	35
4. Neighbours	BBC1	Tuesday	34
Neighbours	BBC1	Wednesday	34
6. Coronation Street	ITV1	Monday	26
7. Count Duckula	ITV1	Tuesday	25
Top of the Pops	BBC1	Thursday	25
9. EastEnders	BBC1	Thursday	24
EastEnders	BBC1	Tuesday	24
Blind Date	ITV1	Saturday	24
Beadle's About	ITV1	Saturday	24
13. Challenge Anneka	BBC1	Friday	23
Bread	BBC1	Sunday	23
15. Disney Club	ITV1	Sunday	22
Jewel of the Nile	ITV1	Sunday	22
Bravestar	BBC1	Monday	22
18. Romancing the Stone	ITV1	Sunday	21
Catchphrase	ITV1	Saturday	21
Coronation Street	ITV1	Friday	21
Coronation Street	ITV1	Wednesday	21
Grange Hill	BBC1	Friday	21

Source: AGB/DMB&B Media.

around 4 p.m. when children return from school and child programmes are shown. However, children are still available to view
well into the evening: some 50 per cent view through to 8 p.m., and
30 per cent view after 9 p.m. and 2 per cent are still viewing at
10 p.m. Moreover, research suggests that they are not passive
viewers who simply watch what their parents choose. Children are
extremely important in determining which programme and therefore which channel is viewed, not just during traditional child time
but also late into peak viewing.

ITV succeeds with the child audience during breakfast time with
TV-am. In the station's early days the appearances of the legendary
puppet, Roland Rat, attracted children and subsequently their parents, thereby solving TV-am's apparently irreversible audience and
financial problems. TV-am now secures two-thirds of the breakfast-
time audience with expenditure from child-targeted advertisers still
forming the backbone of its revenue. Early child-time programming
has produced encouraging performances and the recent introduction

TABLE 2
Top Children TVR Programmes – Excluding Repetitions
October 1989

Programme	Channel	Day	TVRS
1. Neighbours	BBC1	Monday	38
2. Coronation Street	ITV1	Monday	26
3. Count Duckula	ITV1	Tuesday	25
Top of the Pops	BBC1	Thursday	25
5. EastEnders	BBC1	Thursday	24
Blind Date	ITV1	Saturday	24
Beadle's About	ITV1	Saturday	24
8. Challenge Anneka	BBC1	Friday	23
Bread	BBC1	Sunday	23
10. Disney Club	ITV1	Sunday	22
Jewel of the Nile	ITV1	Sunday	22
Bravestar	BBC1	Monday	22
13. Romancing the Stone	ITV1	Sunday	21
Catchphrase	ITV1	Saturday	21
Grange Hill	BBC1	Friday	21
16. Birds of a Feather	BBC1	Monday	20
The Bill	ITV1	Thursday	20
Knight Mare	ITV1	Friday	20
Smash Hits	BBC1	Sunday	20
Ovide	BBC1	Wednesday	20

Source: AGB/DMB&B Media.

of *Home and Away* at 5.10 p.m., as the ITV equivalent to *Neighbours*, has worked well, considerably boosting ITV's share and overall child audience after 5 p.m. However, from 5.30 p.m. ITV's child audience never recovers from the damage inflicted by the regular screenings of *Neighbours* and the BBC maintains its increased audience share into peak-time. The example of *Neighbours* and TV-am suggests that the overall audience is significantly affected by a programme's ability to attract children. (See Table 3.)

If children are important in determining a television company's overall audience performance, what is their significance as consumers? As with children's viewing, there are considerable difficulties in researching children's spending habits: children and teenagers are disparate groups in many respects. Consequently there is not much data to show how much money they have and what they spend it on. However, some research data does exist, conducted by Carrick James Market Research, and its survey for 1987 shows that children and teenagers should be recognised as serious consumers. For example, they estimate that 12–19 year-olds have a spending power of just under £14,000 million per annum. The survey also indicates that

TOTAL HALF HOURLY CHILDREN TVR
ITV & BBC 1 October 1989

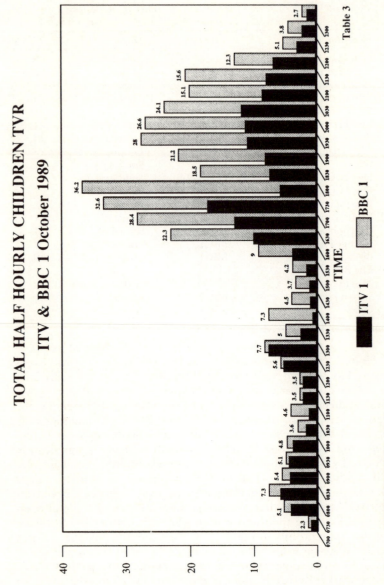

Table 3

Source: AGB/DDS/DMB&B   Media

children spend significant sums of money on a range of products and services including clothes, records and tapes, confectionary and, of course, toys. More interesting, though, is the fact that C J M R has a building society study which shows that three-quarters of 7–19 year olds have a savings account and two-fifths save regularly, even those in the younger age groups. This indicates a 'consumer sophistication' among children.

What is impossible to quantify is the effect that children have on the family's overall spending. But it is generally accepted that they have substantial influence on the purchasing decision when products are bought for their own use, such as food, drinks, clothes and toys, and their influence almost certainly extends to the choice of products purchased for general family use.

Children are important as both viewers and consumers, but inherent difficulties in developing programmes for a broad age range of children and scheduling them effectively in the present I T V networking arrangement indicate that their significance might go unrecognised by commercial television.

The Government White Paper on the future of broadcasting, published in November 1988, expounds the virtues of greater choice. For example, it states that Channel 3 (I T V) should 'provide a diverse programme service calculated to appeal to a variety of tastes and interests' but it is actually very unspecific on how these tastes and interests should be catered for. Indeed it is anticipated that the I T V network, and the new Channel 5 will have greater programming freedom than is currently the case.

The I T V network, in whatever form it is structured from 1992, will have to make a decision between continuing the current nominal service to children and relying on adult programming to pull in a child audience at other times, or developing a dedicated strategy on children's programmes. This would have to cater for all age groups, and would involve running programmes in peak time, as well as the traditional child viewing periods. The former course of action seems more likely on current evidence, but it ignores the prospect of a very different T V environment in the 90s.

The new satellite channels will encounter many difficulties in launching and becoming established, as is already apparent. What will undoubtedly aid their development is the opportunity to identify weaknesses in the terrestrial services and plan their schedule to compete against them. In this respect child programming is I T V's particular Achilles' heel.

Recent Pan-European Television Audience Research (April 1989) surveying viewing in cable and satellite homes confirms this prospect. It shows that the satellite channels' share of total viewing was

25 per cent, but their share of children's viewing was 39 per cent. ITV and Channel 4 may choose to regard this as a not particularly serious problem. This would be short sighted. If the satellite channels can make inroads into their audience through child programming it would have greater implications than just the loss of a few child ratings. Child viewing can and does have a significant impact on the total audience.

It will hardly benefit the long term health of ITV if it allows a new generation of viewers to establish its main allegiance to the satellite channels. Television should be the obvious medium for advertising to children because its creative properties are so powerful. At the moment it is not. Both the quantity and quality of child programming is of a poor standard, and consequently advertising opportunities are limited and costly. As the satellite services become established, this is likely to change. ITV will either have to improve its service to children or be in serious danger of losing both audiences and advertising revenue.

An Audience Worth Fighting For

Reva Klein

Britain is the only country where children's programming has been considered an integral part of the public service broadcasting service provided by television broadcasters since its inception, and where it has been given the commitment and resources to develop into the microcosm of mainstream television. Drama, documentaries, current affairs, magazines, news, animation, quiz and game shows: all are there in the children's slot, as they are in the rest of the schedules. As parents, we may not like all the programmes that are squeezed into the 700 hours of children's programmes on ITV and the 1,000 hours on the BBC this year, but it can't be denied that, with the bad and the indifferent, there is enough good worth saving, even if it means fighting for. BACTV (British Action for Children's Television) is at the forefront of this fight, lobbying politicians and forging links with broadcasters to let them know that parents and children are demanding a continuing commitment to quality programming. Good television, produced especially for children, is important to them.

Why? That question has been asked time and again since the days of *Bill and Ben*, when concerned parents voiced their disapproval of the intruder in the living room irresistibly pulling distracted children from more worthwhile, 'active' pursuits. The role of television in our society, and in children's lives in particular, has been well documented, as David Buckingham suggests above, mainly from a negative perspective. The public has been inundated with reports of how telly-watching has negative effects on the young, how violence on the small screen breeds violence in the playground, how like moving wallpaper it all is. A smaller section of the public has read research refuting these claims, too.

107

Of course we don't want our kids glued to the telly, watching any old thing and picking up nasty role models for hours on end. But they don't watch television in that way. Firstly, again as Buckingham briefly documents, children have fairly rigorous critical faculties, even if they are not always articulated. They know what's daft, what's naff, who represents the moral stand and who does not. Secondly, whether we like it or not, television offers children a common cultural language. Whether it manifests itself in a discussion on what happened yesterday on *Grange Hill* or what they think of the young editor's clothes sense in *Pressgang*, it gives them, and us too of course, something to talk about together, to compare notes on. Thirdly, television opens up children's experience to the inaccessible: wildlife, ecology, fantasy, scientific experiments, drama, different lifestyles, chatting with pop stars. It used to be called broadening one's horizons. That sounds a bit too worthy nowadays but whether it is overtly 'educational' or ostensibly 'fun', at its best children's television allows its viewers to get widely acquainted with the world in which they live.

Unfortunately, the market forces overtaking the ITV companies do not make allowances for the unique and vulnerable place of children in our society. Although everyone is a child for nearly a quarter of their lives, no one going through childhood has a political voice. While we know children are determinedly vociferous critics of just about everything, they lack a true consumer voice except by proxy: their parents. This remains the case even though, as Jim Marshall points out above, those aged twelve and up have considerable spending power. As a sector of the viewing public, children remain a largely problematic homogeneous mass. Although, as David Buckingham says in his article, children aged 8–11 watch more television than almost anybody else, less time is allocated to the children's slot than to their elders' viewing time, and even that time is begrudged by some ITV heads, who stress the lack of cost-effectiveness in 'squandering' money on such a poor 'minority' sector of the viewing public.

David Elstein predicts that without an IBA-style regulatory body to oversee the scheduling, and the time and money spent on children's programming, TV executives will cut as many corners as they can. To make programming cost-effective under the increasing pressure of reduced budgets, while no longer having to fulfil any obligations to this age group, children will lose the quota specifically produced for them.

Kids won't go hungry, the argument is likely to be. Let them eat *EastEnders* and *Blind Date*. After all, everyone knows they prefer *Neighbours* to *Blue Peter* and *Coronation Street* to *Sooty*. There will be market-led programming for children, and to get an idea of what that looks like we need look no further than the legendary awfulness of American examples. There, network broadcasters seem dedicated to the proposition that children are not worth spending money on, ladle out a gruel-like diet of low-quality cartoons and sitcom re-runs for after-school and weekend viewing. This is where deregulation and the profit *über alles* ethic leads. The exception to the American rule, PBS, spends as much time on the air begging for viewers' contributions as it does transmitting *Sesame Street* and other quality shows, many of them from the UK.

Could this be the fate of the BBC who insist that for them ratings are not as important as quality even if the licence fee were to give way to subscription. But David Elstein's grim scenario of a BBC dragged down by a steady stream of cheap programmes, with home-grown animation on ITV, was echoed in an interview with the Head of Children's BBC, Anna Home: 'With no quality competition, we will go cheap, too. We'll fall down with them.'

How can we be assured that this does not happen, that the new franchise holders will voluntarily establish their own standards and formalise a commitment to protect and develop children's programming in the absence of a tighter regulatory body? How can broadcasters be convinced of the crucial distinction between quantity and quality, that filling an hour and a quarter's slot with mediocre material may in fact be no better than leaving a screen blank? Marshall suggests that the sensible way forward is to persuade ITV executives that television is a key advertising medium for targeting children.

It is true that children are not only spenders but are even bigger dupes to advertising ploys than their parents. But if TV executives are persuaded only by arguments such as Jim Marshall's, then more's the pity. Why maintaining and developing the diversity and quality of existing children's programmes should be translated into bloodless marketing terms says a lot about the evolution, or degradation, of this country. Since the post-war period when the infrastructure for a more equal, caring society was built, a great shift in social values and thinking has taken place.

If children aren't our future, what is? If their needs are forgotten in the scramble for profits and ratings then this government and today's broadcasters will have to bear the responsibility for an impoverished television service for our children.

Contributors

Janet Willis is a Project Organiser in the BFI Television and Projects Unit.

Tana Wollen is Education and Research Officer in the BFI Research and Information Division.

David Morley is Lecturer in Communications at Brunel University.

Giles Oakley is a producer in the BBC Community Programme Unit.

Alkarim Jivani is Broadcasting Editor of *Time Out* magazine.

Barbara Vickers is a lone parent with three children. She is an active member of Gingerbread, a self-help organisation for lone parents.

Peter Golding is Professor of Sociology at the University of Loughborough.

Graham Murdock is Research Fellow at the Centre for Mass Communication Research, Leicester.

Samantha Cook is a freelance researcher and writer.

Alasdair Ritchie is Managing Director of Holmes, Knight, Ritchie/WRG Ltd.

Ashwani Sharma is an engineer, at present training in sound at the BBC.

Thérèse Daniels is a Research Officer at the BFI Television and Projects Unit.

Werbayne McIntyre is a Managing Director of WMRB.

Stephen Pegg is a former teacher. His diary, typed with the aid of a head pointer, was the award winning entry for the *One Day in the Life of Television* diary-writing competition.

John Donnelly works for the Scottish National Institute for the War Blinded. He has just completed a BPhil on the War Blinded with the Open University.

Timothy Leggatt is a sociologist and Director of the Broadcasting Research Unit.

David Buckingham is Lecturer in Media Education at the Institute of Education, University of London. He is currently director of an ESRC-funded research project on the development of television literacy.

David Elstein is Director of Programmes at Thames Television.

Jim Marshall is Deputy Media Director of D'Arcy Masius Benton and Bowles.

Reva Klein is a mother of two and a freelance journalist who writes about children's broadcasting and young people's theatre.

Sarah Loveless and **Justine Mooney**, in the BFI Education Department, assisted in the production of this volume.